America's Global Responsibility

America's Global Responsibility

Individuation, Initiation,
and Threefolding

JESAIAH BEN-AHARON

LINDISFARNE BOOKS
GREAT BARRINGTON, MASSACHUSETTS

2004
Lindisfarne Books
P.O. Box 799
Great Barrington, MA 01230
Copyright 2004 by Jesaiah Ben-Aharon

Printed in United States of America.

Library of Congress Cataloging-in-Publication Data

Ben Aharon, J., 1955–
America's global responsibility / Jesaiah Ben-Aharon.—1st ed.
p. cm.
ISBN 1-58420-018-9
1. United States—Social conditions. 2. United States—Economic conditions.
3. Globalization. I. Title.
HN57.B453 2003
306'.0973—dc21
2003009222

Acknowledgments

🖎

THE RESEARCH THAT UNDERLIES THIS BOOK TOOK PLACE during two sabbatical years that my family and I enjoyed in Saratoga Springs from 1998 to 2000. I would like to express our deepest gratitude for the generous support and warm hospitality of our dear American friends that made this possible. Above all, we wish to thank Barbara Glazer and Paul Zachos, Mary Day and Ned Hulbert, Mary and Dave Roberts, Pam and Steve Balmer, Tracy and John MacNeal, John Beck and Walter Alexander. Through them, we were fortunate to experience the best qualities of the American people, and we felt blessed to have the opportunity to become in this way intimately acquainted with the human and spiritual essence of the true being of America.

I wish to dedicate this book to them, and to all Americans who strive to realize America's global responsibility in their daily life, love, care, and spiritual creativity.

Jesaiah Ben-Aharon
Harduf, Israel, April 2003

Contents

𝕎

Acknowledgments v

Preface ix

Introduction 1

Part I
The Shadow of Humanity: Vices of Globalization 19

1. The Great Takeover: How America's Political
   Establishment Became a Tool of Elite Globalization
   (A Short History of the Council on Foreign Relations) 21

2. Old Social Darwinism and New Economy 25

3. Is America Turning into an "80/20" Society? 30

4. The Global Social Situation at the Beginning
   of the Twenty-first Century 35

5. The Asian Economic Crisis 1997–1998 42

6. Survival of the Fittest 53

7. Joseph Stiglitz's Condemnation of the
   "Washington Consensus" 65

8. The 77 Group Meeting at Havana 75

9. The Moral Divide 78

Part II
The Spiritual Origins of Individuation and Threefold
Social Differentiation and Integration 81

10. Threefolding in Historical Perspective 83

11. The Weakening of the Modern State:
    Global Economy Rules the World 93

12. Modern State and Centralized Social Structure 99

13. Civil Society Comes of Age:
    A Global Call to Conscience 108

14. Individuation and Social Decentralization 116

15. Individuation and Modern Initiation:
    The Spiritual Origin of Threefolding 121

16. Synergy Between Social Activism
    and Spiritualized Science and Consciousness 147

17. The Battle of Seattle and its Aftermath:
    Elite Views of Civil Society 153

Epilogue 167

About the Author 180

Preface

❦

The Burden of Power,
The Strength of Conscience

THIS IS, IN SOME SENSE, A BOOK ABOUT "FREEDOM," THAT
delicate possibility that opens the doors to both good and evil.
In Part I of *America's Global Responsibility*, we face the consequences of freedom: the distressing reality that "America" as a
geopolitical force is a platform for the same old ruthlessly
selfish grab for wealth and power—larger in scope and more
sophisticated in means, but no different in character from any
previous example of the disease. In Part II, however, Jesaiah
Ben-Aharon asks the question of real freedom in his carefully
studied reassertion of individual self-development as the
central force at work in human evolution.

This emerging individuality is more than the equal of the
Empire and its "dark side," if only it grows in self-awareness
and finds effective social forms.

Persons devoted to either side of this light-and-shadow
play might claim Ralph Waldo Emerson as their ancestor, born
200 years ago. His great phrase "self-reliance" can be hijacked
to explain "no government handouts" and "unilateral pre-
emptive warfare" and private greed. But Emerson's sinewy
essay *Self Reliance* itself works its way to a final twin assertion,
that:

"Nothing can bring you peace but yourself. Nothing
can bring you peace but the triumph of principles."

This implies an equation of "yourself" with "the triumph of
principles." It sounds wonderful, but what is the reality?

Such a twinship is what Dr. Ben-Aharon unfolds for us. As
a true and often painful self-development of individuals is
taking place around the world—a self-development involving
millions of Americans—so too are consciences being stirred to
affirm principles in every field of social life. *Individuality* of an
increasingly high character appears to be an evolutionary principle in itself, a place where all other principles can appear in
their "self-evidence." And since Americans have always been
notable *doers*, it also appears that painful errors are a necessary part of the education of this people—a people sincere and
naïve, blundering but very open to change.

A native son of Israel, Ben-Aharon has lived and is living
with the struggle between generous idealism and opportunistic
power over others—the struggle which is such a long, red
thread in American life and history. He has experienced the
global power of the United States from its Israeli cockpit and
protectorate in the Middle East, and he sees our challenges
clearly and writes about them succinctly. I think that he is
objectively hopeful for us Americans—from a deep, strong
level of understanding—and I am grateful for the reassurance.

Born of a declaration of self-evident truths, but heavily
mortgaged to self-interest from the get-go, the United States
conducted fearful and profitable deceit toward the "Indians,"
a spiritually mature and often noble collection of nations, gave
people like Emerson their first deep pangs of conscience. The
slow, hard progress of principles continued then with the
African slaves; with each new wave of immigrants; with

women; with laboring people and the poor of the Great Depression; with the civil rights of people of color and with women's broader social rights; with the blithe destruction of Nature; with sexual and affectional difference; with the vast mistreatment of animals.

We Americans have affirmed the individual more and more concretely, and yet we are awakening in the twenty-first century to find ourselves heirs of all the empires and tyrannies of history. The concept of the "corporation" as the legal mechanism for increasing power while reducing responsibility looms large in this titanic, global struggle, which segues into the greatest issue of all—the profit-and-dominance driven, technologically enabled reshaping of human nature itself, from the cells up.

"What shall it profit a man if he gain the whole world and lose his own soul?" Always a famous text for sermons, this question—posed by someone who stood as an utterly self-reliant individual against the absolutist powers of religious authorities and the Roman *imperium*—is becoming an exact statement of the shape of our new manifest destiny, the choice standing before every conscious American. This small volume helps, in Jefferson's phrase, to "inform our discretion."

John H. Beck
August 2003, New York City

Introduction

❦

THE IMAGE OF THE LIVING EARTH BROUGHT HOME TO US BY means of the most advanced American science and technology both reflected and dramatically enhanced the emergence of global consciousness beginning in the 1960s. This change of consciousness was not unlike the cosmic illumination experienced by ancient and modern mystics and initiates as they have sought to contemplate the sacredness of all life and the uniquely vibrant existence of planet Earth in the universe. Only a short historical time after physicalist and positivist metaphysics reduced Earth to no more than another meaningless speck of dust in a meaningless universe, and two world wars and the Cold War dealt a seemingly mortal blow to human hope and future confidence, we have experienced again Earth's and humanity's uniqueness. This dramatic reversal inspired in millions of people a growing sense of love and responsibility to our living planet, and all the beings that live on it. The sight of Earth from space became a profound rite of passage for a whole generation, the globe over:

> Viewed from the distance of the moon, the astonishing thing about the earth, catching the breath, is that it is alive. The photographs show the dry, pounded surface of the moon in the foreground, dead as an old bone. Aloft, floating free beneath the moist, gleaming membrane of bright blue sky, is the rising earth, the only exuberant thing in this part of

the cosmos. If you could look long enough, you would see the swirling of the great drifts of white cloud, covering and uncovering the half-hidden masses of land. If you had been looking for a very long, geologic time, you could have seen the continents themselves in motion, drifting apart on their crustal plates, held afloat by the fire beneath. It has the organized, self-contained look of a live creature, full of information, marvelously skilled in handling the sun.[1]

This new perspective overcomes a deeply entrenched traditional assumption that is a legacy of nineteenth-century materialism: that natural science is inherently inimical to spirit. Some versions of natural scientific thinking, especially since the end of the nineteenth century, have become deeply engrossed in such physicalist belief systems and metaphysics, denying life and consciousness their central role in our existence. But this was, and in some orthodox materialist circles still is, a caricature and travesty of the true spirit of natural science, which embodies openness, wonder, creativity, and ever-deepening and expanding realization of the mysteries of the vast intelligence in which our cosmic becoming is grounded. Thanks to largely American scientific, technological, economic, and political determination, human beings have begun to experience their global home from outside and feel an indescribable "intimacy from afar." We had learned to treat what lies so majestically before our senses all day long as a mere meaningless source for raw materials, and we had to travel far away to rediscover it. This gradually developing expansion of human consciousness is, first and foremost, what is referred to by the term "globalization." The gift of this perspective is undeniably one of the most important contributions of modern science and technology to the positive evolution of human consciousness in our time, and thus humanity owes much to American creative capabilities and daring imagination.

The age of globalization began, therefore, as a result of a wholly justified expansion of humanity's mind and soul forces, its scientific and technological imagination and acumen. Generating and mastering the power that made this cosmic view of Earth available to humanity as a whole, America also shouldered the great opportunity and responsibility to use its immense resources to the benefit of humanity as a whole. It has begun to learn the lessons of power and responsibility, and struggles to expand its interests and make the true interests of others its own concern. But important questions arise. Will the U.S. use its power to increase narrow-minded interests? Will it share its power with other nations and peoples? Will America become powerful and responsible at the same time? It is clear that the natural richness of the American land—taken hold of by the dynamic creativity and industriousness of its people— has given America the unparalleled social power to spread its gifts to other nations and peoples if it so chooses.

The inherent qualities and capabilities of the United States are not difficult to discover. Combined with the immense physical and natural resources of its land is a remarkable dynamism of creative and highly intelligent will power, masterfully capable of using the riches of the earth for the benefit of physical civilization. What was achieved in this regard in 250 years has no precedent in human history. A closer look at the work in progress that is the United States shows that its success originates in the ability not only to discover hidden laws and forces of nature, but above all to marshal and implement them in a well-concerted and integrated, socially productive process. At their best, Americans are capable of mustering and fusing together human intelligence, daring, intuitive imagination, courageous initiative, large sums of capital, and social and political will to achieve real advances in material culture. They can integrate large and manifold social factors, without reducing their mutually enriching diversity into abstract and impoverished unity. These factors are molded into a unified power with a dynamic resolution to carry impulses into action that characterize this nation of otherwise staunch individualists. It is this creative tension between individualism and collective social will, the continuous pulling together and falling apart of the individual and the forces of social coherence, that generates a uniquely powerful momentum and energy that can be projected far and wide.

In this sense we speak about America as the land destined—when the intellectual North Pole and the living, metabolic South Pole shall find their conscious harmonization—for the "renewal of the Mysteries of the living Earth." This renewal takes place when free human beings creatively imitate and, in so doing, transform living nature by learning to marshal nature's own creativity in order to go beyond what nature can realize. In the course of billions of years of free experimentation, nature solved the great riddle of how to make life possible in the physical world. Now, following nature, humans learn and recapitulate, in the shortest imaginable time span, what nature achieved during billions of years, in order to advance nature's goals beyond nature's capacities in a humanized, free, and exponentially rapid acceleration. America's vision is a wholly transformed Earth, shaped entirely by the human, that will bring nature's potential to highest realization, and will spread human intelligence and morality beyond Earth into our solar system and beyond. The United States economy, politics, and cultural-spiritual achievements, past, present, and future, are making these developments available for the benefit of humanity as a whole.

Especially in the United States, it is instinctively felt by each person that human beings are *beings of becoming*. Evolution is both the driving force and the leading ideal that embodies the best western contribution to the evolution of human consciousness—the idea that humanity is evolution becoming conscious of itself and is the growing edge of that evolution, for good and ill. America's inherent spiritual power lies precisely in the incomparable ability of its leading representatives to embody in their will, initiative, and action the universally human, to differentiate it in advanced specializations, and to demonstrate the creative possibilities that arise from the synergy of the "individual" and the "whole."

This was also the driving force behind the so-called "American system" of national economy. The system generated tremendous creative energies during the middle of the nineteenth century and made the United States a world power in the twentieth century. In fact, it made the U.S. into the most powerful nation the world has ever known, a global power that has dominion over the whole planet. However, when hegemony is achieved, the question of power is transformed into a question of ethics and morality—that is, of *America's global responsibility*. The real tests of global power begin the moment hegemony is established, because the U.S. is and will be constantly questioned by the rest of humanity concerning its real motivations. Is the U.S. truly responsible for the "general welfare" (to use a term from the U.S. Constitution) of its own citizens and of the nations and the peoples that now live under its global hegemony?

Since the 1960s and '70s, parallel with America's growing global supremacy, there has been a remarkable and consistent progress in shaping a positive national and global vision and role for America, in the northern and southern hemispheres alike. A closer look at the creatively human, social, and cultural forces in America today shows that they are striving in all domains to shape a positive global vision and role for the United States. Many of the thinkers and doers that struggle to formulate this vision feel inspired by the future prospects of mind and consciousness-transformative science and technology, and by the words of the Founding Fathers in the Constitution and the Declaration of Independence.

They find inspiration in, for example, the following statement, in which, for the first time in human history, a *universal* and spiritual, biblical conception of the human being became a social foundation for a life of a modern state:

> We hold these truths to be self-evident: that all men are created equal, that they are endowed by their Creator with certain unalienable rights, that among these are life, liberty, and the pursuit of happiness.

These profound words taken from the Declaration of Independence give expression to existential values that live in the American people. The words were originally conceived to guide the highest ideals for the social formation of the United States within its own borders. But since the United States has become the leading global power, those same words now oblige it in its conduct towards humanity as a whole. Now they must be taken in their global, even cosmic, sense, using America's global power to ensure the life, liberty, and happiness of all nations and creatures on Earth. The forces that oppose the realization of these ideals in the U.S. itself are the same ones that use America's global power for selfish ends. They are the enemies of the founding goals and vision of the United States, whether inside or abroad, and, under the rubric of protecting "American interests," they merely use U.S. power to foster their own interests and goals. Americans committed to the true vision of their nation are often painfully aware that America's name and ideals are usurped and used in a manner quite contrary to the spirit of the nation's founding documents.

What, then, is America's vision as expressed in the lofty words of the Declaration of Independence? It maintains that it is a "self-evident" fact that all humans are inherently *equal*, and that this endows them with certain *basic human rights*. It also states that these rights are essentially three: the right to life, which can be interpreted to mean the right to a decent economic existence in the physical world; the right to liberty, which means that equality of human nature is the guarantee of free social order or democracy; and the right to the pursuit of happiness, suggesting that a meaningful and creative life is the foundation of a culture worthy of humans. We see here that one central spiritual value, the value of equality, becomes a foundation for realizing human rights in the economic, political, and cultural sectors.

This "threefoldness" is inherent in the Declaration of Independence. If human beings are all created in the image of one God, then their social relationships must be worthy of this assumption. Human rights are essential to the human being and are sacred because they belong to us by dint of our divine nature. Society should reflect these rights in economic life, by allowing each person to meet basic human needs; in the democratic political state, by allowing each person to freely partici-

pate; and in recognizing the right to meaningful life as an
essential human need in the cultural-spiritual sphere.

The words "self-evident" seem to imply that the equality of
all people as sons and daughters of one divine source, of one
spiritual and universal essence of human nature, can be *known*
through direct perception or intuition, a recognition that
pierces like lightning through ordinary intellectual deliberation. It is a matter of intellectual dynamism, a will factor in
cognition, an acceleration of the perceptive faculties, as
Emerson taught us. We must be very quick in order to experience "self-evidence," on whatever level of cognition, because
otherwise our vision will be clouded and weakened, and we
shall doubt our ability to experience it. Before or after the act
of perception, we may practice exact intellectual reflection,
analysis, and careful, slow deliberation. But we should distin-
guish clearly between the two faculties of cognition, and give
each its due, using each for its appropriate tasks.

The American founding intuition also has this implication:
*that each human being realizes his or her self to the extent that
he or she freely perceives the same spiritual essence in other
human beings.* And society should be shaped accordingly,
which means that this concept will find its expression in the
promotion and protection of human rights. As a nation built
on the integration of immigrants from all over the world, the
U.S. is uniquely disposed to synthesize a strong national identity marked by a sense for diversity and the basic equality of
human nature, a sense that must be maintained as the ground
that supports, and is challenged by, this diversity. Respect for
diversity and human equality must also shape the U.S.'s global
role. Within and without, these are the same lessons of power
and responsibility. This is America's vocation.

Admittedly, it can be objected that America's founding documents and their characteristic formulations are still heavily colored by the European liberationist traditions from which they originated historically. However, as we shall see below in greater detail, an original and fresh American spirit is striving to assimilate such historical influences and use them merely as initial models in order to gradually create its inborn economic, political, and cultural realities. In American social life there is a constant struggle, in which the relics of old, abstract ghosts of European intellectualism, operating especially powerfully through the medieval, largely Roman judicial system, are striving to suppress the native freshness of the American spirit. There is no greater enemy to the American spirit than old European intellectualism, especially in its juristic embodiment. On the spiritual-moral level, it destroys one's faith in creative, spontaneous forces of perceptive and active intuition. Socially, it sucks away, like a vampire, any trace of human loyalty and trust. This can be clearly seen in the powerful "special relations" that prevail between Wall Street business, corporations, and law firms, as well as in the all-pervasive infiltration of all walks of American social life by legal and insurance interests. Such relations, however, stand in stark contrast to original American social intuitions.

This can be seen in the unique formulation in the passage from the Declaration of Independence quoted above—an expression that goes beyond the essence of legalism. We refer here to the meaning of the expression "self-evident." The essence of Roman, continental legalism is precisely the implicit denial of any intuitive self-reference to truth and evidence; truth must be mediated, by hierarchies celestial and ecclesial, and "self-reliance" must become inherently unthinkable and undoable. Taken in an Emersonian sense, self-evidence cuts through 2,000 years of dialectics and threatens to make the social domination of legalism superfluous. It seems to imply that the equality of all people as sons and daughters of one divine source, of a common spiritual and universal essence, can be experienced through *creative perception*, or intuition, which operates by means of actual spiritual activity in the living present and presence of the perceived "other." For example, Otto Scharmer's recently formulated self- and organizational transformation process, termed "presencing,"[2] seeks to embody this Emersonian creative intuition, which relegates intellectual analysis and reflection to the secondary, preparatory functions by means of which we can re-present our intuitions, in order to support and ground spiritual activity that takes place in the living present.

In the 1990s, influential American politicians and policy-makers praised America as being the "sole global super-power"(Zbigniew Brzezinski) and the "indispensable nation" (Madeleine Albright). Since September 11, 2001, the neoconservative discourses concerning the American empire, and its nature and functions, have been embraced by American elites in all walks of life. This has meant that at the end of the Cold War, hidden ambitions and agendas can no longer be concealed; the bipartisan American establishment's commitment to world domination is out in the open global field. What is lacking is a positive vision that will show how America can translate this power into true global responsibility for the *whole* of humanity and Earth. This fateful omission is all the more decisive since America emerged for the *third* time as a victor in the last century, winning the Cold War against the Soviet Union. Once victory was assured and global dominion was safely established, it seemed reasonable to expect that the United States would use its immense resources and global power for the good of the whole. However, the collapse of communism brought no essential change in U.S. foreign economic, political, and cultural policy. On the contrary, there has been a consolidation and hardening of hegemonic doctrines, ideologies, and metaphysics between the collapse of communism and today. In 1997, Brzezinski, who had been President Carter's national security advisor, published a remarkably candid field guide for the practicing American imperialist in his book *Grand Chessboard*, in which he openly confessed decades-long expertise in the revival of the Roman arts of geopolitics. Brzezinski, who initiated the anti-Soviet *jihad* in Afghanistan, formulated the idea, now widely shared in Washington, that the U.S. should seek to "prevent collusion and maintain dependence among the vassals, keep tributaries pliant and protected, and . . . keep the barbarians from coming together." In 1993, Samuel Huntington, professor of international relations at Harvard University, gave expression to the U.S. establishment's political ethics, in his "clash of civilizations" vision of perpetual future war of "the West against the rest," in which "western Christian civilization" is founded on the following moral maxim: " 'Unless we hate what we are not, we cannot love what we are' . . . . We know who we are only when we know who we are not and often only when we know whom we are against."[3]

Among the many contributions and variations on Huntington's theme, a book by Robert D. Kaplan of the *Atlantic Monthly* is worth mentioning. Kaplan, who was recently featured at the New York Council on Foreign Relations (CFR) and is being interviewed widely, has written a book entitled *Warrior Politics: Why Leadership Demands a Pagan Ethos*[4]. He argues that the U.S. should play the role of an imperial power, carrying "Churchill's baton," and should apply a pagan (Greco-Roman) morality, which is more oriented toward "outcomes" than the Judeo-Christian ethic. Another promotion in this direction came in the January 12, 2002 "Arts and Ideas" section of the *New York Times,* which featured author Alexander Stille interviewing British journalist Sebastian Mallaby. Mallaby was discussing an upcoming article of his in the CFR journal *Foreign Affairs,* which called for a new imperialism. Stille wrote: "For some strategic thinkers, [September 11, 2001] leads to what might be considered an antique and anti-democratic proposal: empire." He quoted Mallaby's own words: "A new imperial moment has arrived. . . . The chaos out there in the world is too threatening to ignore, and the existing tools for dealing with the chaos have been tried and found wanting." Finally, from London resounded, in the words of the *Economist*'s editor, Bill Emmott, the happy conclusion that America need be "[t]he reluctant sheriff no longer," because:

> Another word, once considered rather daring, is becoming commonplace in policy seminars and on talk-shows: empire. . . . No one has in mind colonies or an emperor. But there is a strong, sometimes hubristic, sense that America has the opportunities, obligations and threats associated in the past with empires: that it can set the rules that govern international relations, while at times operating outside them itself; but also that ultimately it alone can enforce those rules, a role which makes it the prime target of anyone who dislikes them.[5]

On September 20, 2002, the Bush Administration issued its blueprint for global domination and perpetual military interventions in its comprehensive policy statement entitled, "The National Security Strategy of the United States." The National Security Strategy sets forth the American military-industrial complex's ambition for the U.S. to remain the world's superpower, maintaining global political, economic, and military dominance. The stated policy of the U.S. is "dissuading military competition" and preventing any other world entity or union of states "from pursuing a military build-up in hopes of surpassing, or equaling, the power of the United States."

In recent years we have witnessed the expansion of NATO to the borders of Russia, the dismembering of Yugoslavia and the American-led war of NATO against Serbia, a new "great game" in the Caspian Sea region and central Asia, and the endless continuation of the war in the Persian Gulf. Instead of suggesting a global plan for economic reconstruction and social development in eastern Europe, Russia, and Asia, the American political establishment, guided as strongly as ever by narrow-minded and globally irresponsible financial circles (together with their allies in Europe and Asia), is consistently carrying out its elite agenda with no regard to the true mission of America and its responsibility as the hegemonic global power.

The idea of empire is a radical departure from the image (as articulated by nineteenth-century French historian Alexis de Tocqueville, and still applicable today) that Americans have of themselves and their country as a democratic exception among nations. This contradiction is no longer a cause of great concern. Those who still have any scruples, and they are increasingly few, qualify the words "empire" and "hegemony" with adjectives such as "benevolent" or "gentle." Robert

Kagan of the Carnegie Endowment for International Peace writes: "And the truth is that the benevolent hegemony exercised by the U.S. is good for a vast portion of the world's population. It is certainly a better international arrangement than all realistic alternatives."[6]

Despite the globalist and triumphalist image created by American corporate, financial, and political establishments, socially and spiritually mature American civil society and culturally creative people will resist this and become increasingly powerful in formulating and realizing America's true vision and mission in the age of globalization.

It is America's karma to learn the lessons of power. This destiny can only unfold over the course of several centuries. However, at certain periods in America's history an effort, at least, was undertaken by certain leading individuals, inspired by "the true Mysteries" of America, to provide a vision of Americanism not limited by the social, political, and economic establishments of the time. In such brief periods, it seems as if a different American spirit shines through from behind the scenes of world events, and tries to bring national and global evolution into a certain harmony with the true goals of humanity's evolution.

Franklin Delano Roosevelt's social policy after the Great Depression, and his largely unrealized foreign policy intentions after the end of World War II, can serve as a certain example of such a rejuvenation of the original American social and cultural mission, both toward its own citizens and in practicing its world dominion in responsible ways. FDR understood that only an honest realization of and adherence to the essence of the Declaration of Independence could rescue the American people from the horrendous social collapse brought about by the collapse of the economy following 1929, a collapse insti-

gated by the unscrupulous financial practices of the elite financiers who ruled the United States in those days. At the same
time he was striving to use American supremacy in order to
help the defeated countries and the rest of the developing
world. Roosevelt, like John F. Kennedy, following in his foot-
steps in the 1960s, began to formulate the foundations for an
American role in the world that would be in accord with the
Declaration of Independence. Roosevelt struggled hard with
the globalists and imperialists of his time, at home and abroad.
The intensity and meaning of the conflicts between FDR and
Churchill, the true father of Anglo-American imperialism of
the second half of the twentieth century, are played down and
neglected by mainstream historians. However, according to
FDR's son, Elliott, in his book *As He Saw It*,[7] Roosevelt was a
strong anti-imperialist. Elliott even goes as far as to claim that
his father considered Great Britain and its imperial system to
be far more dangerous to the U.S. than was the Soviet Union.

Elliott offers some evidence to support such seemingly
unacceptable notions. The following description of a major
confrontation between the two leaders is instructive. Elliott
recounts that the first serious clash reported by Roosevelt took
place in Argentia bay, Newfoundland, in August 1941, at the
discussions accompanying the drafting of the Atlantic Charter,
which was to formulate the democratic principles of the
western free world. Elliott writes that while Churchill began to
explain the significance of British Trade arrangements,

> Father broke in. "Yes. Those Empire trade agree-
> ments are a case in point. It's because of them that
> the people of India and Africa, of all the colonial
> Near East and Far East, are still as backward as they
> are."

Churchill's neck reddened and he crouched forward: "Mr. President, England does not propose for a moment to lose its favored position among the British Dominions. The trade that has made England great shall continue, and under these conditions prescribed by England's ministers."

"You see," said Father slowly, "it is along in here somewhere that there is likely to be disagreement between you, Winston, and me. I am firmly of the belief that if we are to arrive at a stable peace, it must involve the development of backward countries and backward peoples. How can this be done? It cannot be done, obviously, by eighteenth-century methods."

"Who's talking about eighteenth-century methods?"

"Whichever of your ministers recommends a policy which takes raw materials out of a colonial country, but which returns nothing to the people of that country in consideration. Twentieth-century methods involve bringing industries to these colonies. Twentieth-century methods include increasing the wealth of a people by the standard of living, by educating them, by bringing the sanitation—by making sure that they get a return for the raw wealth of their community. . . ."

"You mentioned India," he [Churchill] growled.

"Yes. I cannot believe that we can fight a war against fascist slavery, and at the same time not work to free people all over the world from a backward colonial policy."

Unfortunately, Roosevelt died suddenly on April 12, 1945 without being able to implement his far-reaching ideas. The Marshall Plan for the reconstruction of Europe, the Bretton Woods organizations—the World Bank and the International Monetary Fund—and later the United Nations are hegemonic and globalist distortions of some of his far more universal-human ideas. Another American President, John F. Kennedy, strove to continue FDR's inner social policies and international strategies, adapted to the needs of America and the world in the early 1960s. But his career was cut short.

Since September 11, 2001, Americans have become aware of their country's vulnerable and porous borders. This awareness can be used negatively, in order to procure more security and tougher emergency rules and to increase its capacity for global military intervention. Or, conversely, this vulnerability can be seen as an opportunity to learn basic lessons of power and responsibility. This is America's vocation. Can this vocation be realized in practical economic, political, and cultural ways? In order to answer this question, we have to delve deeper and locate the place in which the true American spirit is connected to the true goals of the evolution of humanity and the cosmos.

Rudolf Steiner realized as early as 1919 that Germany's military and political situation expressed a much deeper social and moral collapse, and that America was going to become the new global empire. But will America learn the moral responsibility that comes with power? This means actualizing freedom, equality, and brotherhood in modern social life:

> The Anglo-American element may well achieve world dominion, but without the threefold ordering

of society this dominion will flood the world with
the death of culture and the sickness of culture.[8]

Notes

1. Lewis Thomas, *The Lives of a Cell: Notes of a Biology Watcher* (New York: Penguin USA, 1997), p. 170.
2. For a collection of Scharmer's writings on "presencing" visit the Generon Consulting Website at www.generonconsulting.com.
3. Samuel P. Huntington, *The Clash of Civilizations and the Remaking of World Order* (New York: Simon and Schuster, 1996), pp. 20–21.
4. New York: Vintage, 2003.
5. Bill Emmott, "Present at the Creation," *Economist*, June 27, 2002.
6. Robert Kagan, "The Benevolent Empire," *Foreign Policy*, Summer 1998.
7. Westport, CT: Greenwood Pub. Group, 1974.
8. Rudolf Steiner, *Ideas For a New Europe: Crisis and Opportunity for the West* (Great Barrington, MA: Anthroposophic Press, 1996), p. 49.

Part I

The Shadow of Humanity:
Vices of Globalization

Chapter 1

The Great Takeover: How America's Political Establishment Became a Tool of Elite Globalization

(A Short History of the Council on Foreign Relations)

IN THE TWENTIETH CENTURY THE UNITED STATES OF AMERICA became, to quote Zbigniew Brzezinski, a "first and only global superpower," controlling world affairs to an extent not possible for any former world empire. In what direction are we to turn our gaze in order to find the forces that led the United States to a one-sided global hegemony? One such direction is described below.

The only existing official account of the history of the Council on Foreign Relations (CFR), written by Peter Grose,[1] begins with the following description:

> The Inquiry . . . to the select few who knew, this was the name of a working fellowship of distinguished scholars, tasked to brief Woodrow Wilson about options for the postwar world once the Kaiser and imperial Germany fell to defeat. Through the winter of 1917–18, the academic band gathered discreetly in a hideaway at 155th Street and Broadway in New York City, to assemble the data they thought neces-

sary to make the world safe for democracy. . . . The
vision that stirred the Inquiry became the work of
the Council on Foreign Relations over the better part
of a century: A program of systematic study by
groups of knowledgeable specialists of differing ideological inclinations would stimulate a variety of
papers and reports to guide the statecraft of policy-
makers.

"We are skimming the cream of the younger and more
imaginative scholars," declared Walter Lippmann, the 28-year-
old Harvard graduate who recruited the scholars and managed
the Inquiry in its formative phase. "What we are looking for is
genius—sheer, startling genius, and nothing else will do."
    When the young scholars, who accompanied Wilson to the
Paris Peace Conference at Versailles in 1919, returned they first
proposed, with a group of British colleagues, a permanent
Anglo-American Institute of International Affairs, with one
branch in London, the other in New York. (As it turned out,
eventually the British and the Americans each established their
own independent institutes.)
    However, the story of the Versailles academic group is only
one part of the founding story of the CFR. Deeply involved in
the political maneuvers that reshaped the map of Europe and
indeed the whole planet before, during, between, and after the
two world wars were interested and forward-looking American businesspeople, financiers, and lawyers. They had a vital
economic interest in the outcome of World War I and in the
shape of the coming new world order, and strove to navigate
American foreign policy in a manner conducive to their
purposes. It was precisely this *coming together* of business and
academic research that made for something new. Peter Grose

describes ". . . a more discreet club of New York financiers and international lawyers" that, meeting for the first time in 1918, called itself the Council on Foreign Relations. "It began with 108 members, high-ranking officers of banking, manufacturing, trading, and finance companies, together with many lawyers. Its purpose was to convene dinner meetings, to make contact with distinguished foreign visitors under conditions congenial to future commerce."

Both groups found that they had much to gain from a mutual, cooperative venture. The financiers provided funds, and the Versailles academicians supplied diplomatic experience and academic expertise. This synergy, says Grose, "whether to promote business expansion, world peace, or, indeed, both . . . produced the modern Council and promoted its unique utility for decades to come: academic and government expertise meeting practical business interests, and, in the process, helping conceptual thinkers to test whether they stood on 'rock or quicksand.' " The phrase "whether to promote business expansion, world peace, or, indeed, both" must be read carefully in order to appreciate the full significance of the founding of the CFR.

On July 29, 1921, a New York certificate of incorporation was prepared and the new Council on Foreign Relations came into being. This new and unique compact forged between international American finance and business groups, strongly supported by Wall Street lawyers, distinguished by influential representatives of all branches of the mainstream academic and political establishment, fostered an intensity of social coherence unknown before in human history. It marshaled for the twentieth century those forces in the U.S. that assume that the pursuit of the financial interests of American companies and corporations serves the highest good of the American people and of humanity as a whole—and, therefore, that such pursuit must actively be made into the main goal of American domestic and foreign policy.

The power that made the American-based corporate and financial powers into the backbone of a global superpower is grounded in this unequaled achievement.

Will this power be wielded, one day, for the greater benefit of the American people and the peoples of the world? Until now, unfortunately, the new spiritual-moral forces in America have not been strong enough to change the destructive course of elite globalization—that is, of the processes described above: the centralization and merging of the three sectors of society, economy, and polity, forming a power regime. Elite globalization is the exact opposite of the modern ideal of threefolding, which aims at the free cooperation between decentralized and clearly differentiated sectors of society. Seen in this light, this project of elite globalization is the greatest hindrance to universal development of freedom, equality, and brotherhood.

Let us take account of a more recent expression of the basic worldview that lies behind the elite project described above. Then we shall study its effects on the American and global social situations.

Notes

1. Peter Grose, *Continuing the Inquiry: The Council on Foreign Relations from 1921 to 1996* (New York: Council on Foreign Relations Press, 1996).

Chapter 2

Old Social Darwinism
and New Economy

IT SHOULD BE REMEMBERED THAT THE IDEAS ARTICULATED BY the American spokespeople noted below have little to do with the social values, practice, and spirit inherent in the foundation and purpose of the United States. On the contrary, such opinions and deeds stand in sharp contradiction to true American ideals and values. Furthermore, the fact that we concentrate below on the American aspects of elite globalization should not lead us to believe that elite globalization is a purely American phenomenon. However, this book is concerned particularly with the United States and its unique position as the nation with the most power to do harm or good, and the sources cited below reflect this focus.

The following is a typical example of the views prevalent among the movers and shakers of elite globalization. On May 10, 2000, U.S. Treasury Secretary Lawrence Summers addressed the Hambrecht & Quist Technology Conference in San Francisco. The title of his speech, "The New Wealth of Nations," borrowed from Adam Smith's 1776 book, though not without a certain historical irony, since Smith wrote his *Wealth of Nations* mainly as a political treatise to discourage the Americans from rebelling against imperial Mother England. Indeed, empires come and go. And today the Amer-

ican people and land pay a heavy social price for the aspira-
tions of international oligarchs who exploit the American
nation for their definitely non-American goals.

Summers praised the "new economy" in the United States
in hyperbolic terms: "America is the most fortunate country in
the world. This is as fortunate a time to be an American as any
in our history. And those involved in the high technology
sector stand out in their good fortune relative to other Americans."

Summers then developed at some length the already well-
known arguments concerning the merits of the "new" (high-
tech) economy as opposed to the "old" (industrial) economy. I
do not wish to imply that those arguments are not true "in
themselves," because the new high-tech inventions and practices are transforming economy and society as a whole.
However, I wish to point out that these arguments are often
highly questionable, and their results are economically and
socially one-sided. This imbalance plays out in strong, destabi-
lizing local and global socio-economic effects, especially as the
basic function and importance of physical or classical economy
are marginalized. Of course, the inflated stock bubble burst
eventually, as was all too obviously going to happen all along,
bringing about an economic recession in the U.S. and globally.
A more responsible endeavor would have been to find precisely
the right relationship between "old" and "new" economies,
and to establish a rational relationship between them. Such an
approach, however, is very rare nowadays.

For example, Summers took the well-trodden path,
preaching to the convinced one to ten percent of the American
population for whom the "global Casino" (to use economist
David Korten's fitting phrase), administered from Wall Street,
the City of London, and other elite financial centers, became in

recent years a source of unimaginable wealth. I cannot recall any other time in human history, except perhaps the later, decadent days of the Roman Empire, in which leading elite powers were so unresponsive to and irresponsible in the execution of their global duties as in the last decades of the twentieth century and the beginning of the twenty-first. If we look at the overall economic, social-human, and cultural costs of this present extravagance, well hidden by American mainstream "free media" from the eyes of most Americans (who, on their part, choose of course to remain in this state of blessed ignorance), we will discover symptoms of long-term regression in most basic areas of American society in comparison to the levels reached in the 1960s and '70s. We notice that basic economic indicators are lagging far behind the largely artificial economic "boom" of recent years. Most parameters show non-renewal of general economic infrastructure, deterioration of agricultural production and farm maintenance, decreased food and industrial manufacturing quality, and the precipitous decline of most basic social services and welfare in America, especially in medical care and education.

The Treasury's celebrated macroeconomic and monetary strategies, mutually coordinated with Federal Reserve chairman Alan Greenspan's fiscal policy, created a wholly irresponsible, super-overheated, and fantastically unreal collective "pyramid game," the worst to take place in human history. The speculative stock bubble that financed this American global deficit economy was, according to the prophets of the new economy, a more or less true reflection of its new strengths.

Summers contended that the "old industrial output" of "physical products" is becoming marginal, while "increasingly today the canonical product is a gene sequence, a line of computer code or a logo." The "old" economy is a "negative feedback economy," controlled by a "Newtonian system of checks and balances." The "new" economy, according to Summers, increasingly will be a "positive feedback economy, one in which rising demand drives higher efficiency, and higher returns drives lower prices and yet higher demand. In such a world, the avalanche, rather than the thermostat, becomes the more attractive metaphor for economic policy."

The not-so-new social moral behind most of this comes out eventually, when Summers says that actually, "[t]he right metaphors for the new economy are more Darwinian, with the fittest surviving, the winner frequently taking all, and, as modern Darwinians have come to understand, accidents of history casting long and consequential shadows."

As former World Bank chief economist Joseph Stiglitz points out (see below), Summers represents those elite circles for whom the suffering of millions will always be, in Darwinian terms, justified, if the chosen few—the fittest—are prospering. This is the reason why he can praise deregulation and the role of markets and "the spur of competition" in the post-industrial age—trends that guarantee that the U.S. will continue to benefit enormously from the digital revolution, as well as from a ". . . national financial system that makes America the only place in the world where you can raise your first $100 million before you buy your first tie." In Summers's typical elite worldview, there was no stock bubble, no monstrous private and corporate debt accumulation, no expanding American current account deficit, and no giant backlog in U.S. investments in the public infrastructure.

Let us take a glance at another spokesman of the same ethics, chosen from the daily press. Under the May 10, 2000 headline "An Unlimited Stock Market," a leading *Washington*

Post columnist, David Ignatius, celebrates the American economic "success" of the last ten years. In some peripheral places outside of the flourishing U.S. civilization, he writes, there is still a predominant fear of adopting "American-style risk-taking" in "Wild West" stock market investments, but he is sure that this will soon be changed. "[W]hat the rest of the world could use," apparently, ". . . is a few more people like Michael Milken, the man whose 'junk bonds' blew apart the old, staid system of corporate finance in the United States." And though he mischievously admits that Milken was "a little too creative—criminal in fact," Milken "helped create the conditions for America's explosion of wealth and creativity during the 1990s." Before turning to the rest of the world, it is worth asking how this accumulation of wealth is distributed among the citizens of the United States.

Chapter 3

🪶

Is America Turning into
an 80/20 Society?

THERE IS NOTHING MORE INIMICAL TO THE AMERICAN PEOPLE than elite globalization. Unfortunately, the same elites have been highly successful in the last 100 years in harnessing the creative power of the American people for their own purposes. Only in this way can we explain the paradox that "Americanism" has become a *bad word* around the globe, while, at the same time, American society itself is suffering from the same symptoms as many other nations, caused by the same truly anti-American and anti-human forces. However, this fact is not known to most Americans—any more than they know about the effects of the elite globalization that is taking place in the name of "Americanism" throughout the rest of the world.

The hard numbers collected and presented in what follows can be eye openers to anyone seriously interested in the true state of the American people and society in the last 30 years. Late in 1999, the Census Bureau of the U.S. Department of Commerce reported in its publication "Money Income in the United States, 1998" that in 1998, American families earned the highest level of income in U.S. history. This is offered as proof that America is in the tenth year of an "economic boom." On closer inspection, the Census Bureau report actually shows that the U.S. economy is contracting. The total income of American families did reach a record level, as the Census Bureau alleges. However: 1) the greater portion of that increase came from purely financial gains (capital gains, interest, stocks) and had nothing to do with real economic growth; and 2) most of the income increase went to the families in the upper 20 percent of the income bracket. In fact, the report showed that the U.S. has become a "two-tier society," in which the upper 20 percent sucks in the lion's share of income each year, while the real living standard of the remaining 80 percent is continually declining. Meanwhile, America's staggering internal debt and its enormous trade deficit continue to balloon.

The income gap has widened steadily over the last two decades. In 1977, the lower 80 percent of families earned 55.8 percent of America's total after-tax real annual income. The growth of the speculative bubble and the contraction of the physical economy caused a profound transformation over the next 22 years. By 1999, the upper 20 percent of families earned 50.4 percent of America's total after-tax real income; the lower 80 percent earned only 49.6 percent of this total. The upper 20 percent of families had more total income than the entire lower 80 percent of families, which totaled 92 million families and approximately 221 million people. Also, the upper 1 percent of families alone (1.2 million families, representing 2.75 million people) took in more income than the lower 38 percent of families (43.7 million families, representing 105.6 million people). This was the highest income discrepancy in U.S. history. The main income stream that has bolstered the incomes of the upper 20 percent is that of realized capital gains. Two other, purely financial sources of income also grew greatly during this 22-year period: personal dividend income and personal interest income.

Between 1955 and 1990, realized capital gains grew slowly, but stayed within a fairly moderate band, usually far below $200 billion (with the exception of 1986). Beginning in 1990, they started to rise at a faster pace. Then, between 1995 and 1999, realized capital gains leapt from $180 billion to an estimated $530 billion, tripling in only four years. Thus, between 1995 and 1999, the increase in realized capital gains alone was $370 billion. Three-quarters of this went to the upper 20 percent of the population.

By 1999, realized capital gains had reached an estimated $530 billion, and personal dividend income and personal interest income were approximately $174 billion and $787 billion, respectively. The combined total of all three sources plus some other categories of capital income amounted to a staggering $1.61 trillion. Of this $1.61 trillion, 75 percent, or $1.2 trillion, flowed to the upper 20 percent of families.

The income arising from realized capital gains has now risen to 21.3 percent of America's personal income. It is a larger percentage of total personal income than the income of the productive labor force (manufacturing, construction, mining, agriculture, transportation, and energy generation), which has been reduced to 18.5 percent of total income.

But even these figures do not fully represent the growing disparity in living standards between the upper 20 percent and the lower 80 percent, because they do not reflect the collapse in infrastructure in the communities where most people live. That collapse includes, for example, the lack of sufficient medical facilities, the breakdown in transportation systems, and the steep decline in the quality and quantity of education. In 1963, for example, the cost of a new home amounted to the equivalent of 399 weekly paychecks for an average non-agricultural worker. By 1998, the cost had risen by 91 percent, to 761 weekly paychecks. The average worker's purchasing power, in terms of purchasing a new home, had fallen by 48 percent.

The upper 20 percent of families are able to earn the largest share of America's income because they hold the greatest share of the nation's income-generating wealth. In fact, the divergence between the upper 20 percent and lower 80 percent of households is even larger in terms of net wealth than in terms of income. The wealthiest 10 percent of U.S. families own 70 to 90 percent of all of America's stocks, bonds, estates, trusts, other (non-primary residence) real estate, and futures contracts. The upper 10 percent own more than 90 percent of privately owned (non-public) businesses, giving them basic control of hard physical assets, including oil, gas, and other energy supplies, food supplies, and the hard infrastructure for communications. This wealthy layer is also accumulating substantial portions of the stock in publicly owned companies engaged in the same hard-commodity activities. The wealthy own the lion's share of precious metals, in the form of gold bullion and jewelry. It is to a significant extent true, what some have said openly: This upper 10 percent "owns" America.

In 1995, according to the Federal Reserve "Survey of Consumer Finances," U.S. families held stocks worth a total of $2.75 trillion. Of that amount, the super-wealthy 1 percent held 42.2 percent, or $1.16 trillion worth; the next 9 percent of families held 42.2 percent, or $1.16 trillion. In contrast, the lower 90 percent of U.S. families held only 15.6 percent, or $0.43 trillion of stocks. Since the upper 10 percent of families held 84.4 percent of all stocks, it is no mystery that three-quarters or more of all realized capital gains, as well as personal dividend income, flowed to those families. The situation is even more extreme for bond and business holdings. In 1995, the nation's families held bonds worth $1.14 trillion. Of that, the wealthiest 10 percent held 90.3 percent, and the remaining 90 percent of families held only 9.7 percent. At the same time, the businesses owned by U.S. families had a total worth of $4.02 trillion. Of that, the wealthiest 1 percent held 71.4 percent, or $2.87 trillion; the lower 90 percent held a mere 7.7 percent.

In terms of total wealth, the lower 90 percent of families in 1995 held $6.473 trillion or 31.5 percent of America's wealth, while the upper 10 percent of families held more than double that, namely $14.046 trillion, that is, 68.5 percent. In addition, in 1995, the super-wealthy 1 percent of families (representing 2.75 million people) owned more of America's wealth—35.1 percent—than the lower 90 percent of families (representing 247.5 million people), whose share was 31.5 percent. This is the greatest disparity in wealth in the United States since 1929.

The one area dominated by the lower tier of the U.S. population is debt and liabilities. The lower 90 percent of America's families holds 70.9 percent of the total liabilities and debt of American families. The enormous debt burden of America's lower 80 percent of families has been built up because those families have had to borrow in order to make up for lost buying power.[1]

The concentration of American wealth in the hands of such a small group is evidence of a misuse of American power and creativity—only the elite reap the benefits. Such an imbalance in an increasingly small world, in which all peoples are intimately interconnected, can only lead to social disasters, and has so far led the world into the great catastrophes of the twentieth century and already, dangerously, shaped the global social situation at the beginning of the twenty-first century.

Notes

1. *Executive Intelligence Review*; see also: The Center for Budget and Policy Studies at www.cbpp.org.

Chapter 4

❦

The Global Social Situation
at the Beginning of the
Twenty-first Century

THE GLOBAL SITUATION AT THE BEGINNING OF THE TWENTY-first century shows the dire social results of more than 100 years of the predominance of one-sided, elite-directed economic development of the North American and western European powers—at the expense of basic cultural, political, and economic human needs, interests, and values in these powerful countries and in the world as a whole. The tendency of modern economic development to override other basic needs of society is inherent in its historical moment; that is, in its increasing emancipation from the theocratic, feudal, physiocratic, and class-binding social forces by which it was bound until the eighteenth and nineteenth centuries. This emancipation is not incidental or wrong in itself; it is a necessary and fully justified development from the perspective of the general individuation of human consciousness in the course of recent history. As such, it is a part of the driving force that leads the independent human soul toward a fuller understanding and utilization of the forces and materials of the physical world, and at the same time develops its unique human, social, and cultural-spiritual faculties.

But this development is not without its dangers. One is that a reversal of means and goals takes place, and the intensive development of the physical means of living obscures the real reasons for their development. Instead of development for the sake of the human, lives are spent in unworthy conditions in order to satisfy unlimited desires for more power—and for entertainment, whose function now becomes to fill the emptiness caused by the suppression of the human soul, mind, and spirit. This danger is undoubtedly real, and what is more, it is also existentially necessary. After all, why should we yearn for radically new developments in human evolution and expect to be spared its possible aberrations and risks? In each new evolutionary stage the good cannot be a given—it must be striven and fought for. For example, in a wholly new stage of social integration, as in the new global age, the misuse of economic power to create inhuman life conditions for billions of fellow human beings awakens and spurs us to greater responsibility and creativity. Without this impetus, we wouldn't have developed the real strength needed for *free* moral initiative and action—the only kind that will be helpful in the future. Hence, evil is beneficial in the long run; it is, as Faust realizes, "part of that power in the world, that ever evil seeks and ever good achieves," a power that seeds evil but lets maturing human forces harvest a greater good.

The social results of elite globalization are by now well documented. These include the influence of global economy on our ecological systems:

The global output of goods and services grew from just under $5 trillion in 1950 to more than $29 trillion in 1997, an expansion of nearly sixfold. From 1990 to

1997, it grew by $5 trillion—matching the growth from the beginning of civilization to 1950. . . .

As the economy grows, pressures on the Earth's natural systems and resources intensify. From 1950 to 1997, the use of lumber tripled, that of paper increased sixfold, the fish catch increased nearly five-fold, grain consumption nearly tripled, fossil fuel burning nearly quadrupled, and air and water pollutants multiplied several-fold. The unfortunate reality is that the economy continues to expand, but the ecosystem on which it depends does not, creating an increasingly stressed relationship.[1]

While economic indicators such as investment, production, and trade are consistently positive, the key environmental indicators are increasingly negative. Forests are shrinking, water tables are falling, soils are eroding, wetlands are disappearing, fisheries are collapsing, range lands are deteriorating, rivers are running dry, temperatures are rising, coral reefs are dying, and plant and animal species are going extinct. The Worldwatch Institute, quoting environmental writer Edward Abbey notes:

"Growth for the sake of growth is the ideology of the cancer cell." Just as a continuously growing cancer eventually destroys its life-support systems by destroying its host, a continuously expanding global economy is slowly destroying its host—the Earth's ecosystem.[2]

What is most alarming about the global economy is that it has created a growing polarization in most economic parame-

ters between poor regions, nations, and populations, and the
rich ones:

> Globalization offers great opportunities—but only if
> it is managed more carefully and with more concern
> for global equity.
>
> Proceeding at breakneck speed but without map
> or compass, globalization has helped reduce poverty
> in some of the largest and strongest economies—
> China, India, and some of the Asian tigers. But it has
> also produced losers among and within countries. As
> trade and foreign investment have expanded, the
> developing world has seen a widening gap between
> winners and losers. Meanwhile, many industrial
> countries have watched unemployment soar to levels
> not recorded since the 1930s, and income inequality
> reach levels not recorded since the last century.

- The ratio of global trade to GDP has been
  rising over the past decade, but it has been
  falling for 44 developing countries, with more
  than a billion people. The least developed countries, with 10 percent of the world's people,
  have only 0.3 percent of world trade—half their
  share of two decades ago.
- More than half of all developing countries have
  been bypassed by foreign direct investment,
  two-thirds of which has gone to only eight
  developing countries.
- The terms of trade for the least developed countries have declined a cumulative 50 percent over
  the past 25 years.

- Average tariffs on industrial country imports from the least developed countries are 30 percent higher than the global exports in industrial nations.

The share of the poorest 20 percent of the world's people in global income now stands at a miserable 1.1 percent, down from 1.4 percent in 1991 and 2.3 percent in 1960. It continues to shrink. And the ratio of the income of the top 20 percent to that of the poorest 20 percent rose from 30 to 1 in 1960, to 61 to 1 in 1991—and to a startling new high of 78 to 1 in 1994.[3]

The United Nations Human Development Reports of 1998 and 1999 show a powerful continuation of all the above trends. The 1999 Report finds that "global inequalities in income and living standards have reached grotesque proportions":

While 1.3 billion people struggle to live on less than $US 1 a day, the world's richest 200 people doubled their net worth between 1994 and 1998 to more than $1 trillion. The world's top three billionaires alone possess more assets than the combined Gross National Product of all the least developed countries and their combined population of 600 million people.

About 840 million people are malnourished, and close to one billion find it difficult to meet their basic consumption requirements. More than 880 million people lack access to health services, and 2.6 billion people have no access to basic sanitation.

Far from narrowing, the gulf between rich and poor is growing:

> The income gap between the fifth of the world's population in the wealthiest countries and the poorest fifth of the world's population was 74 to one in 1997, up from 60 to one in 1990, and 30 to one in 1960. Those living in the highest income countries have 86 percent of world Gross Domestic Product (GDP), 82 percent of world export markets, 68 percent of foreign direct investment and 74 percent of world telephone lines. Those living in the poorest countries share only one percent of any of these.
>
> OECD countries, with 19 percent of global population, control 71 percent of global trade in goods and services, and consume 16 times more than the poorest fifth of the globe.[4]

The following details may be added: Today, 358 billionaires enjoy an income level equivalent to that of 2.4 billion (2,400,000,000) of the world's poorest. Further, of the largest 100 economies of the world, 51 are transnational companies, or TNCs. These TNCs are economically larger, in terms of turnover, than over 140 countries of the world. And it has been said that a few hundred TNCs control 70 to 80 percent of world trade.

Are such imbalances necessary? Many in leading corporate, financial, and political circles consciously believe so. My point of view is different. I believe that it is *not* necessary, not even as a temporary by-product of modern evolution, but that it represents a conscious intellectual and moral *choice* on the part of individual human beings. The process of individuation, as we shall show, can lead also to a very different social situation for humanity that will reflect an entirely different set of choices, values, and decisions. There is absolutely nothing deterministic and inevitable in the radically imbalanced and destructive social situation at the beginning of the twenty-first century, just as there was nothing deterministic about the great catastrophes and tragedies of the last century.

Human beings like you and me are shaping the face of human society and planet Earth by means of our daily conduct, according to our ideas, values, circumstances, and personal desires. The decision to blame others, nature, nurture, fate, or perhaps the weather is but another conscious choice. Human ideas, moral values, and decisions are the stuff that underlies the current global social situation. Let us look more closely at some of them and their results.

As we do so, please understand that my purpose in reporting these facts is not to agitate for this or that political or social ideology or world conception. My purpose remains phenomenological throughout. But we need to know what our fellow human beings are experiencing and thinking today around the globe. Global ignorance was never as dangerous as today. In order to be truly *informed*, we must go beyond our particular cultural and social milieu and realize to what extent our "free society," as our "free market," is only free for a very selective spectrum of *the total human experience and existence of humanity as a whole.*

Notes

1. *State of the World 1998: A Worldwatch Institute Report on Progress Toward a Sustainable Society* (New York: W.W. Norton and Company, 1998).
2. Ibid.
3. *Human Development Report 1997* (New York: United Nations).
4. *Human Development Report 1999* (New York: United Nations).

Chapter 5

☙

The Asian Economic Crisis
1997–1998

LET US BRIEFLY BE REMINDED OF THE GREAT ECONOMIC CRISIS that hit Asia in 1997–98: the collapse of currencies—more than 30 percent in Indonesia's case—and financial institutions from Thailand to South Korea to Japan; an unprecedented $57 billion bailout of the Korean economy by the International Monetary Fund; the agreement signed in Geneva by 102 nations committing Asian countries to open up their financial markets; the decision of Japan, under heaviest U.S. pressure, to open up its humbled banking industry to western banks—these are some of the dry facts. But do we remember some of the typical reactions from the side of the "winning powers"? Let us be reminded of some of these, too.

"Asia's Financial Foibles Make American Way Look Like a Winner," announced a front-page headline in the *Wall Street Journal* on December 8, 1997; "Asia's Surrender" read the front page of the *New York Times* six days later. American financiers had been deeply concerned in the 1970s and '80s to see the meteoric rise of the "Asian tigers," whose collective economic output had reached half of the world output and was threatening—if it continued to increase at the same pace into the twenty-first century—to dominate the global market very soon. The crisis changed this situation overnight.

As the *Wall Street Journal* noted, the IMF bailout forced the government of Seoul—the most formidable young "tiger" to have emerged in Asia by that time—"to accept a sweeping set of structural changes that would begin to dismantle a Japanese-style financial system *and replace it with American-style capitalism*." The *New York Times* pointed out that "the United States clearly sees a chance to use Asia's crisis to score some economic points and some philosophical ones as well."

The emergency performances of the International Monetary Fund together with the U.S. Treasury during the Asian crisis could not be kept hidden from the public. Even those who are not critical of the IMF acknowledge that it is "essentially a proxy for the United States" and is controlled by the U.S. Treasury Department.[1] In fact, as Karin Lissakers, U.S. Executive Director of the IMF, testified to General Oversight Subcommittee of the House of Representatives Committee on Banking and Financial Services on April 21, 1998, the representatives of member countries rarely vote—there have been 12 votes in the last 2,000 decisions.

For example, in April 1997, U.S. Treasury Secretary Robert Rubin headed a meeting in which the finance ministers of the Group of Seven (known as G-7, the world's seven largest industrialized democracies), came out with the recommendation to promote "freedom of capital flows" and urged a revision of the IMF charter in order to make the IMF the leading force in this maneuver. This meeting signaled the end of Asia's economic rise, and the beginning of the decisive crisis. The rest is simply a historical record, written large and clearly in all the documents detailing the Asian crisis, as Joseph Stiglitz recounts in his "insider" story from which we will quote below.

The victory cries from the leading American papers will be better understood if we remember that not long ago, during most of the 1970s and '80s, the "Asian economic miracle" had been understood by many leading corporate and financial circles as a possible beginning of the end of the western economic hegemony. In the early 1970s, President Nixon commissioned Peter Gary Peterson to lead a special commission to assess why the U.S. position in the global economy was deteriorating. The report published by the committee showed the U.S. losing ground against Europe and Japan. Ending the report was an appendix titled "The Japanese Economic Miracle," describing the Japanese economic model and contending that it was destined to win the day.

Peterson's book was the beginning. A veritable flood of literature followed, with each book outdoing the one before it in its prophecies concerning Japan and East Asia's rise to global economic hegemony in 20 years, at the most. A new edition of the British economist Andrew Shonfield's book *Modern Capitalism* (first published in 1965) made clear that the Japanese model was not at all that new, and drew attention instead to the dirigiste (national) corporatist model upon which Germany and France based their economic success. In this model, the government plays a major role in developing the necessary economic infrastructures for business. In such corporatist societies it is understood that the government is a leading partner with business and is responsible for most of the basic investments that bring about industrial evolutions and market growth.

In the above-mentioned book, Shonfield further suggested that the corporatist model should replace the Anglo-American system, because it was proving itself to be more adaptable to globalized markets and competition. And indeed, as others have pointed out, in the 1980s and '90s South Korea, Taiwan, and other Asian countries imitated the Japanese version of corporatist capitalism and achieved great success. Not only that, but the IMF, World Bank, and U.S. officials never tried to maintain that these "Asian tigers" were success stories because they followed Anglo-American capitalism; rather, writes Robin Hahnel of American University, "the evidence is overwhelming that successful Asian economies during this period in fact pursued a corporatist, not a laissez faire strategy."[2]

With the onslaught of the Asian crisis, many voices were raised (and not just in Asia) in justified protest, condemning the monetary and fiscal policies of the West. Nicholas Kristof, who covered the Asian crisis for the *New York Times*, wrote:

> Many experts believe that one of the most far-reaching consequences of the Asian financial crisis will be a greatly expanded American business presence in Asia. The United States insists that the main beneficiaries of open markets will be local residents, and the U.S. is not a predatory beast forcing its companies on Asia. But not everyone agrees. There is a growing backlash against what some nations regard as an American model of laissez faire capitalism, which rescues Connecticut hedge funds but sacrifices Indonesian children.[3]

Chalmers Johnson is President of the Japan Policy Research Institute in San Diego. As a knowledgeable authority on the causes of the Asian crisis, he offers a radical assessment of the role that western elites played in instigating and manipulating its course. Some of his controversial ideas were published in the *Los Angeles Times* in June 1999, in an article titled "Let's Revisit Asia's 'Crony Capitalism' Economy: America's Free Trade Proselytizing is the True Root of What is

Now a Global Crisis."⁴ He reveals that behind the curtain of
misinformation spread by elite news networks, there circulates
a very different version concerning the causes of the Asian
crisis. This version "is developing in seminar rooms from Seoul
to Kuala Lumpur to Beijing," in places that many western and
Asian elite circles prefer to ignore as long as possible. There it
is common knowledge, and indeed a consensus, that "with the
end of the Cold War, the United States decided it had to launch
a rollback operation in East Asia if it was to maintain its global
hegemony. The high-growth economies of East Asia had
become the main challengers to American power in the region,
and it was time they were brought to heel."

The campaign worked in two phases. The first was an ideological attack. World-renowned professors of economy began
to preach the gospel of "free markets," the importance of globalization, free flow of capital, and direct foreign investment.
The "Washington Consensus" was becoming a global policy
that included "total laissez faire, destruction of unions and
social safety nets, staffing of regulatory agencies with retired
financiers, indifference to the pay differentials between CEOs
and the ordinary work force, moving manufacturing to low-
wage areas regardless of the social costs, and totally unregu-
lated flows of capital in and out of any and all economies."

The second phase began the actual practical work. In the
moment that Asian economies were beginning to "deregulate"
and dismantle their social and political safety nets, foreign
exchange controls and other protecting measures, "the 'hedge
funds' were let loose on them." These huge accumulations of
hot capital owned by the wealthy elite, especially in North
America and western Europe, have an almost unlimited power
to take over, disrupt, and manipulate financial markets everywhere, while remaining hidden and socially accountable to no

democratic government. "Deregulated" national economies in Asian countries became easy prey for these latter-day global pirates, as they "easily raped Thailand, Indonesia and South Korea and then turned the shivering survivors over to the IMF, not to help the victims but to ensure that no western bank was stuck with 'nonperforming' loans in the devastated countries."

Such a way of speaking is of course unpleasant, and definitely not politically correct. We might have quoted other and more polite sources. For example, Muthiah Alagappa, a Malaysian scholar at the East-West Center in Honolulu, expressed the same basic views in this way: "The Asian crisis obviously strengthens the position of American companies in Asia." Jusuf Wanandi, head of a research institute in Jakarta, Indonesia, is more alarmed: "All our stocks and companies are dirt-cheap. Foreigners may take over everything." And Prime Minister Mahathir Mohamad of Malaysia has said, "If we are not careful we will be recolonized."[5]

Why should one deny what is proclaimed openly? Aren't power politics and power economics the hard core of realistic modern politics? Don't we teach the doctrine to our students in our universities, and isn't it practiced by our diplomats and international organizations as a matter of course, ever since Prince Metternich, former U.S. Secretary of State Henry Kissinger's great ideal and hero, became its founding father at the beginning of the nineteenth century? And hasn't Zbigniew Brzezinski sworn for half a century by the geopolitical doctrines of the father of modern British imperialism, Harold Mackinder (as any cursory look at Brzezinski's manual for twenty-first century American global imperialism, *The Grand Chessboard*, will show)? Who will seriously deny this in theory? And yet who ever admitted this in praxis, when again and again the results are becoming all too apparent?

Of course, the economic and political are going hand in hand with the military. A recent Pentagon study discusses U.S. military affairs and future visions concerning the U.S. military stand in the Asia-Pacific region. This report could alert us to new global adventures and dangers. America's military vision and future projections of its strategic interests and plans in the Asia-Pacific region should be noticed especially in the light of what was said above concerning American economic bias in this region, not to mention the all-too-prevalent anti-Americanism that swells everywhere but is only seldom reported in the United States.

Thomas Ricks writes in the *Washington Post* that in this still unreleased document, titled "Joint Vision 2020," the Pentagon envisions Asia instead of Europe as the prime focus of the U.S. military in the coming decades. It identifies China as a "peer competitor," and projects an indefinite military presence in Korea and Japan, even if the "threat" from North Korea disappears.

Ricks reports further that the Pentagon is consolidating a new strategically based political framework for the U.S. military's "re-entry in Southeast Asia." For example, he writes, the U.S. has strengthened its military relationship with the Philippines, under the so-called "Voluntary Forces Agreement." This arrangement, in which "U.S. forces will conduct frequent joint exercises to train Americans and Filipinos to operate together in everything from disaster relief to full-scale combat," is believed to be a possible model for Southeast Asia as a whole.[6]

Military, political, and economic concerns—these are the more or less well-coordinated aims of one and the same globalization policy. If we turn again to the economic arm, and listen to the testimony of Jeffrey Garten, now dean of the Yale

School of Management, we may have fewer doubts that the conditions that gave rise to American business ascendancy in Asia were not unplanned or accidental. In a revealing statement to Nicholas Kristof (in the *New York Times*, February 16, 1999), Garten recalled that when he was a high-ranking official in the Commerce Department and a key member of the neoliberal "attack" team:

> We pushed full steam ahead on all areas of liberalization, including financial. I never went on a trip when my brief didn't include either advice or congratulations on liberalization. Wall Street was delighted that the broad trade agenda now included financial services. There wasn't a fiber in the bodies of Mr. Rubin, Mr. Kantor, and the late Commerce Secretary Ron Brown— or in mine—that didn't want to press as a matter of policy for more open markets wherever you could make it happen.

Kristof makes it clear that Asia was chosen particularly for "the push for financial liberalization," because it was a "potential gold mine for American banks and brokerages." Three administrations and five presidential terms had labored to prepare the rich Asian gardens: Reagan's two terms, then Bush's four years, and Clinton's eight. Now it was ready for the great end-of-the-century harvest. Finally, Japan was forced to agree to a "big band" opening of its capital markets, which meant that American companies could finally come down on Tokyo in order to have their share of the $10 trillion Japanese personal savings capital market. When the big Japanese brokerage firm Yamaichi Securities collapsed and Merrill Lynch took over many of its branches the harvest was fully reaped.

In the increasingly delicate and unstable global economic, social, and national environments, such remorseless behavior is simply the most direct way to a far vaster global disaster. We urgently need leaders who can rise today to understand the "good of the whole," and not of this or that part, strong or "central" as this part may be. A positive global synergy is as possible in the twenty-first century as its very opposite—an escalating global nightmare of power struggles on a completely different scale than what we experienced even in the bloody twentieth century.

An Asian reaction, even if slow and hesitant, will surely come, and instead of the global cooperation that should be the western contribution to the present and future evolution of humanity, we will witness a continuation of struggle and strife, in a much more complex and precarious global social situation.

In a speech and interview given to the Thai newspaper *The Nation* during the first week in May 2000, in the context of the early May "ASEAN [Association of Southeast Asian Nations] plus Three" meeting in Chiang Mai, former Japanese Vice-Finance Minister Eisuke Sakakibara, one of the key inspirers of the Chiang Mai agreements, declared that "nations rise and fall, and American hegemony is by no means permanent." He added, "What we have learned from the East Asian crisis is that the so-called 'Washington consensus,' leaving the resolution of the problem completely to free market and proper macro-policies, did not work. . . . In fact, except for the brief period of August 1998 to early 1999, U.S. financial institutions and the U.S. economy have gained significantly from the Asian crisis."

The time had come, Sakakibara said, for Asian nations, instead of simply waiting for the next crisis "that may really hit at the center," to "build defensive mechanisms to shield us." Given such defensive mechanisms, "countries could or, perhaps, should, opt for the market economy with partial capital controls depending upon their size, developmental stage, and their social and political constraints." Moreover, countries should, besides implementing "limited currency controls," come to agreements on how to pool currency reserves in a regional framework such as an Asian Monetary Fund (AMF). Sakakibara noted that, in September 1997, the Japanese government had proposed the creation of an AMF. The initiative had failed to go ahead, he said, because, it was "strongly opposed by the U.S. and European countries on the ground that it would undermine the discipline imposed by the IMF."[7]

While such voices are increasingly heard around the globe, a most narrow-minded and dangerous, indeed, utterly cynical approach to human life is rampant in the leading circles of elite globalization. The fact that even late in 1998, IMF's managing director Michel Camdessus could describe the Asian crisis as a "blessing in disguise," according to the *Wall Street Journal* (September 24, 1998), is evidence of this. Why should we then be surprised if more and more students of—and experts on— the global social situation of humanity in our time reach more or less "radical" opinions? Haven't many of the leading persons and organizations that support elite globalization done their utmost in recent years to justify them?

Notes

1. Michael Wines, "Yeltsin Agrees to Closer Ties with Belarus," *The New York Times*, December 26, 1998.
2. Robin Hahnel, "The Question of Imperial Intent," *Z Magazine*, September 9, 1999. Much of this chapter's analysis owes a great debt to this article.

3. See Nicholas D. Kristof, "Asia Feels Strain at Society's Margins," *New York Times*, June 8, 1998. See also: Kristof, "Asia's Crisis Upsets Rising Effort to Confront Blight of Sweatshops," *New York Times*, June 15, 1998; also illuminating is David Sanger, "Decisions by U.S. and IMF Worsened Asia's Problems, the World Bank Finds," *New York Times*, December 3, 1998. Quoted in Hahnel, op. cit.

4. *Los Angeles Times*, June 25, 1999.

5. Quoted in Hahnel, op. cit.

6. Thomas Ricks, "Changing Winds of U.S. Defense Strategy: Pentagon Is Shifting Attention to Asia," *Washington Post*, May 27, 2000.

7. See also, Eisuke Sakakibara, "Is Asian Recovery Sustainable?" Asian Development Bank, 2000, 33rd Annual Meeting Seminar, in Chiang Mai, Thailand, May 2000.

Chapter 6

Survival of the Fittest

Africa and Latin America

FOR MOST OF THE POORER COUNTRIES OF THE WORLD, THE opening up of their economies in the last two decades has coincided with a sharp decline in their rate of growth. Income per person in Mexico, for example, increased by 3.9 percent annually in the 1960s and 3.2 percent in the 1970s; since 1980, it has been stagnant. The figures are similar for Latin America as a whole.

It is important to understand what an enormous difference this makes in people's living standards. When per capita income grows at a rate of 3.9 percent per year, it means that the average person's income will double in about 18 years. For the average Latin American, income has gone nowhere over the last 18 years. This means that for an entire generation, the poor—who constitute the majority of the population in many Latin American countries—have lost the chance to improve their living standards. And this does not even take into account the increased inequality in the distribution of income; in Mexico, for example, workers' real wages have fallen below their level of the 1970s, and have continued to fall sharply over the last three years in spite of rapidly growing productivity.

For Africa, the era of globalization has been even more disastrous, with per capita incomes actually falling. A recent report issued by the World Bank, prepared jointly by the United Nations and African development institutions, admits that life conditions in sub-Saharan Africa are worse today than they were in the 1960s. According to a *New York Times* article from June 1, 2000, apart from very few countries, "AIDS, malaria, and civil strife" are on the rise throughout the continent.[1] The study reveals that sub-Saharan Africa is the only major region in the world that actually *moved backward* in the last third of the twentieth century (compared only to the devastation that Russia experienced in the 1990s through the combined policies of the IMF, the World Bank, and the United States Treasury, as we shall see below).

We may be moved to open our eyes and hearts to Africa's reality when we learn that the total economic output of the 47 nations of sub-Saharan Africa is only marginally greater than that of a little state like Belgium.

Russia

Murray Feshbach, a research professor at Georgetown University, is one of the few Russian "experts" who are not afraid to spell out clearly the true Russian state of affairs. He is heeded in discussions that deal with the horrendous social effects of elite globalization and U.S. foreign policies on Russia in the last decade of the twentieth century. In an article published in the *Washington Post* ("A Sick and Shrinking Nation," Sunday, October 24, 1999), he briefly summarized some basic results of his researches on the subject. Below we reproduce some elements of his study.

"If demography is destiny," Feshbach begins, "then the destiny of Russia for the next 50 years is appalling." He goes on to cite the following statistics on Russian population decline. In the mid-1990s, the population of Russia was 148.3

million. By 2015 it is expected to be as low as 138.4 million, and could perhaps drop as low as 131 million. In fact, given some more recent statistics and projections on fertility rates, the lower projection seems more likely, given the anticipated higher mortality rates as losses from the epidemics of tuberculosis and AIDS manifest themselves after 2005. Taking this information together, as well as other factors, a projection of 80 million by 2050 is quite possible.

Feshbach adds that "some 75 percent of all pregnant women in Russia have a serious pathology during their pregnancies," not only from malnutrition, but also from increases in diabetes, endometriosis, and sexually transmitted diseases (other than HIV/AIDS). Infertility appears to be increasing by more than three percent per year, over and above the 15 to 20 percent of all couples who are infertile at this point in time, and syphilis is fast reaching epidemic proportions. An old enemy of Russia, tuberculosis, is making an ominous comeback as incidence is expected to increase to "one million cases by 2002—and cases of multi-drug resistant TB, which now number around 30,000, can be expected to overwhelm the health care system." At the same time, Feshbach says, the incidence of AIDS is rapidly increasing, with two million projected HIV/AIDS cases expected by 2002.

Feshbach estimates the costs of treatment for these ill persons to be close to $30 billion. However, the economic, political, and cultural situation projected for the first decade of twenty-first-century Russia gives very little reason for hope that these funds will be available. With these diminishing fertility rates, Feshbach warns, "GDP will fall and less money will be available to improve the health of the smaller number of women producing healthy babies for the labor force and armed forces." If "restive areas" in the Russian empire should choose this time to seek more autonomy, he concludes, the center may not be able to hold the republics together—a situation that would be more, not less, dangerous for its region and the world.

Trade and Social Disaster

The immense social cost of globalizers' free trade ideas and practices is usually not covered by the mainstream media in North America and western Europe, or by their elite counterparts in the developing countries. However, it is well studied elsewhere. Only the most staunchly socially irresponsible among us can still ignore the suffering of billions because of the unmitigated selfishness of the elite few—and of all of us who live a rather comfortable life as we collect our shares from the rich spoils of their sumptuous, predatory global meals.

Even the most cursory study of the social disasters inflicted on Mexico through the North American Free Trade Agreement (NAFTA) can teach any unbiased observer some basic lessons concerning the use of free trade, including GATT (the General Agreement on Tariffs and Trade) and the World Trade Organization (WTO), to promote elite globalization. Below we will show, using as an example the Mexican-U.S. border region of Ciudad Juarez, some of the devastating social results that, implemented at large on a global scale, are inherent in all aspects of the free trade agenda. Here we can study a clear example of what the global social situation will look like if the World Trade Organization agenda becomes the blueprint for the regulation of the whole spectrum of the economic-social relations between the rich North and poor South.

The 1994 North American Free Trade Agreement helped create jobs for more than 1.2 million Mexicans—250,000 in Ciudad Juarez—churning out consumer products for the biggest name brands in the world. In a convergence of supply and demand, both foreign firms and Mexican workers flocked to Juarez, drawn by the same thing—the wages being offered to workers—but for different reasons. Ciudad Juarez offers $4-a-day jobs in the *maquiladoras*, or assembly plants, founded and run by U.S. Fortune 500 companies that virtually took over the Mexican side of the Rio Grande. This wage was at once higher than elsewhere in Mexico and more than ten times less than the $5.15 minimum wage for an hour's work across the border in the United States.

Mexico now has 3,485 maquiladoras, which translates loosely as "places for making industrial products." All maquiladoras are built for profit. They have low labor costs, no independent unions, and no requirements to meet U.S. Occupational Safety and Health Administration standards.

In this manner, "free trade" becomes a free haven of social unaccountability for multinational American corporations. Here they can be freed from some hard-won advances in American social life. In the poor global South they prolong colonial traditions under new names. Legislation that is socially binding in the United States, covering, for example, labor unions and environmental and health standards, often representing social struggles lasting 100 years and more, are suppressed in the target countries for a long time to come.

Some of the tragic results of this are evident in Ciudad Juarez. Over the last four decades, as its population has more than quadrupled, Ciudad Juarez has also created a market for drug traffickers, migrant smugglers, gun runners, and car thieves. With the criminals has come an explosion of violence and some of the highest homicide rates in Mexico. Sometime in the early 1990s—police cannot say why or exactly when—the pattern of killings changed. Once confined mostly to drug feuds, brawls, and gang fights, the slayings began to include large numbers of women and girls. These new victims were furnished in part by the global economic forces so vital to Juarez's boom. The majority of the slain women worked outside the home; many were migrants whose pursuit of twenty-first-century jobs had created a new phenomenon of mobile, independent, and vulnerable working women, many living away from their more traditional rural communities for the first time. Of those victims who were employed, an estimated 40 percent worked in maquiladoras.

The killings of women, young female teenagers, and many girls in Ciudad Juarez is just one corner of a vast terrain of social devastation that is spreading like brushfire behind the missionary zeal of free trade agreements, through which the Clinton-Gore administration secured its firm corporate and Wall Street support through the 1990s. Buses filled with migrants arrive every day in Ciudad Juarez from all over Mexico. They have pushed the city's population to more than 1.2 million—or as many as 2 million according to other estimates. Most newcomers are impoverished—farmers with land too worn out to provide for their families; economic refugees from the poorest pockets of the Mexican states of Oaxaca, Veracruz, and Durango; thousands of women and girls who have never held a job beyond cooking, washing, cleaning, and accommodating their fathers and husbands.

These people could and should have been integrated from the beginning through local community development programs that implement what we have known now for many decades, but rarely implement: that organic, gradual economic measures must be carefully undertaken if we wish to truly help a developing society to move ahead during the most precarious phase—transition from older to more modern socio-economic formations.

Instead of truly promoting the best social practices to the developing world, industrialized countries export the worst. These practices are destroying the lives of millions of Mexican families all over the country. The same social capital that could have been wisely and constructively used to offer farmers a chance to renew and modernize their local communities and economies, is ripped off as profit by socially unaccountable corporations.[2]

The Children of the World

To the list that includes the overall degradation of ecosystems, increased poverty, and deterioration of human rights, we must add as an especially acute symptom the general decline in the ability of children to enjoy proper childhood. Of course, the meaning of the term "proper childhood" is not universally agreed upon, and may be controversial among many supporters of elite globalization, who see a "proper childhood" in terms of the spread of mass consumerism and low quality mass media and entertainment. However, some facts may still speak their own language.

According to the United Nations, malnourishment could stunt and handicap an estimated one billion children worldwide by 2020 unless a more focused nutrition campaign is launched. In a report released by the Commission on the Nutrition Challenges of the Twenty-first Century, the U.N. says 30 million underweight babies are born every year, resulting in stunted growth and mental impairment. There are more than 150 million underweight preschool children around the world and another 200 million stunted children.

The report labeled South Asia as the hardest-hit region, followed by sub-Saharan Africa, the Middle East, North Africa, Latin America, and the Caribbean. It may be surprising to some, however, that the children of America's closest ally, the United Kingdom, also demonstrate the effect of social Darwinism.

The United Kingdom has one of the worst records on childhood poverty in the industrialized world, according to a June 2000 study by the United Nations Children's Fund (UNICEF). Nearly 20 percent of its young people live below the poverty line, the report says, noting that the U.K. fails on five key indicators of childhood poverty. The childhood poverty rate is high, as is the number of single parents in poverty, the number of jobless households, and the number of people who have low wages or benefits.

Of 19 countries surveyed, the United Kingdom came in fourteenth, just above Italy and below such countries as Hungary, Turkey, and Poland. By contrast, Sweden, Norway, and Finland have rates of child poverty below five percent.

Interviews with families by the London *Observer* reveal that children are eating main meals consisting of toast, beans, and rice pudding. Poor nutrition leads to health problems and poor performance at school, says the *Observer*, adding that many children live in homes with moisture running down the walls and inadequate heating. It is estimated that the U.K. will need to spend more than £15 billion to eradicate the problem. "It is a question this country must face," said David Piachaud, an expert in childhood poverty at the London School of Economics. "Do we want another generation of children who are brought up in poverty, who have worse health, worse education, worse housing and deficient lifetime prospects?" he asked.

According to the *Observer*, U.K. Chancellor Gordon Brown is preparing to introduce new measures to address the problem, including an early childhood program and a fund for youth up to age 19.[3] While the UNICEF report praises measures introduced to alleviate child poverty by 2020, saying that they will cut the poverty rate by one-third and lift one million children out of poverty, it also warns that one-third of Britain's children will remain in poverty even if everyone who is eligible to work finds a job. "Many children will continue to depend on state benefits that currently leave them well below the poverty line," it adds.[4]

Feast and famine are aspects of one and the same illness of today's global civilization; overfed and over-affluent children in rich societies and cultures are at risk for other types of problems. For example, a report published in the *Journal of the American Medical Association*, conducted by researchers at the University of Maryland, raises serious concerns among pediatricians. It found a 50 percent increase between 1991 and 1995 in the number of children aged two to four who were prescribed psychiatric, behavior-changing drugs such as Ritalin and Prozac. It is extremely troubling that young children are being prescribed drugs that have serious side effects and that have never been studied in that age group. These toddlers could prefigure a future peopled entirely by lifelong drug users who have no internal resources for dealing with stress or sadness.

Finally, all over the world, more than 100 million children have to fend for themselves because of poverty, war, and the loss of their parents from AIDS, says UNICEF. Carol Bellamy, head of UNICEF, has said, "Be it in the West or the developing world, we are confronting grave problems in the violation of children's rights. . . . We want to put a face on this crisis, rather than just have people feel sorry for the little children."

Whether orphaned by disease, abused by adults, or stolen for profit, the world's children are increasingly growing up without the love and security of a family and outside the protection of the state—and are denied the basic rights due to any child, the organization says.

The UNICEF report cited above identifies poverty as the major reason why more children are facing a future alone. "It is estimated there are more than 3 billion people in the world who live on less than $2 a day," Bellamy said. "Half of these are children and half of those are living on less than $1 a day. . . . Such poverty takes a toll on children's health and ability to attend school. These children often become ones who are most exploited."

Examples cited by the UNICEF committee's report include a baby abandoned on a doorstep, a girl sent to perform menial work in someone else's household, a boy sent alone to town with a one-way ticket, and a teenager in detention. Such children are regularly found in Africa, Asia, Latin America, and central and eastern Europe, the report said. "Their aloneness is a child rights emergency every bit as serious as the neglect, abandonment, and exploitation which children growing up alone frequently experience." The report further notes that this phenomenon "is just as common and just as pernicious, although often obscured by atrocities and other gross abuses of child rights that attract instant attention."

Are We Living in One and the Same World?
Now let us compare the above with the way Bill Emmott, the editor of the *Economist,* sums up the twentieth century. What the conservative representatives of elite globalization and the new economic world order think about the world situation seems to be millions of light years from reality. The very fact that such divergence of judgment is possible today should be enough in itself to convince us that something is indeed fantas-

tically wrong in the (elite) belief that we have already achieved anything approaching one world, one humanity in a global village:

> The *fin* of this *siècle* has been an astonishingly posi-
> tive period, far more positive than most people in the
> 1980s, and certainly the gloomy 1970s, would have
> thought possible. Liberty—political, economic and
> personal—has become a widespread fact for the first
> time. The threat of war casts its dark shadow over a
> smaller proportion of the world's population, and
> fewer people live in constant fear of arbitrary arrest,
> torture or worse. Too many still do. Nevertheless,
> Franklin Roosevelt's four freedoms—from fear and
> from want, and of belief and of expression—are
> possessed by more people, more securely, than ever
> before.[5]

This reads like the most famous quote from Voltaire's *Candide*: "All is for the best in the best of all possible worlds." Or perhaps the latest conceited statement from a believer in the eighteenth-century Enlightenment idea that human progress is inevitable, that all problems are solvable by reason, and that mankind is forever chipping away at new frontiers. Or maybe the blinkered view of a pampered member of a western elite who waves aside with an airy generalization the vast problems and privations encountered by millions of people.

As a matter of fact, it seems that all that is left to do is simply to affirm positively the cynical last sentence, which demonstrates the depth of the ideological commitment in certain elite circles. As long as such hardhearted convictions prevail among the powerful—and no one who knows their origins and goals will be inclined to believe that they are going to disappear soon—the global social situation described above will continue to worsen. These circles, luckily, no longer represent the only voices among the global elite. As we shall be able to show, among the powerful some unmistakable stirrings of global responsibility have begun to appear, an important one of which is Joseph Stiglitz's wholesale rejection of the fundamentals of the Bretton Woods system and the ideology of the "Washington Consensus"—decided by U.S. economic officials, the IMF, and the World Bank—on poor countries, which constituted the main power base of the elite globalization project in the second half of the twentieth century.

Notes

1. "World Bank Cites Itself in Study of Africa's Bleak Performance," by Joseph Kahn, *New York Times*, June 1, 2000.
1. For an account of one individual's suffering behind the facts, see, "Irma's Dream: Life and Death on Mexico's New Frontier," by Molly Moore, *Washington Post*, June 25, 2000, the first of two articles on the subject.
2. Kamal Ahmed, *Observer*, June 11, 2000.
3. Nicholas Timmins, *Financial Times*, June 12, 2000.
4. Bill Emmott, "On the Yellow Brick Road," *Economist*, September 9, 1999.

Chapter 7

Joseph Stiglitz's Condemnation of the "Washington Consensus"

AS IF WISHING TO SUPPORT THE DEMONSTRATORS AGAINST THE meeting between the World Bank and the International Monetary Fund in Washington D.C., in April 2000 the former chief economist of the World Bank, Joseph Stiglitz,[1] wrote a special article in the *New Republic* (April 17, 2000) in which he openly offered an insider impression of the operation of the International Monetary Fund from his position in the World Bank. This is a unique document, a true insider testimony. The article, entitled "The Insider: What I learned at the world economic crisis," begins in the following remarkable way:

> Next week's meeting of the International Monetary Fund will bring to Washington, D.C., many of the same demonstrators who trashed the World Trade Organization in Seattle last fall. They'll say the IMF is arrogant. They'll say the IMF doesn't really listen to the developing countries it is supposed to help. They'll say the IMF is secretive and insulated from democratic accountability. They'll say the IMF's economic "remedies" often make things worse— turning slowdowns into recessions and recessions into depressions.

And they'll have a point. I was chief economist at the World Bank from 1996 until last November, during the gravest global economic crisis in a half-century. I saw how the IMF, in tandem with the U.S. Treasury Department, responded. And I was appalled.

Stiglitz reflects on the causes of the global economic crisis that began in Thailand on July 2, 1997. He points out that the crisis began after decades of prosperity, brought about by the "economic miracle" of the East Asian "tiger" economies:

[I]ncomes had soared, health had improved, poverty had fallen dramatically. Not only was literacy now universal, but, on international science and math tests, many of these countries outperformed the United States. Some had not suffered a single year of recession in 30 years.

Stiglitz implicates the Washington Consensus, which prop-agated unlimited deregulation, privatization, and free market policies in trade, freeing floods of hot speculative money that created economic and social havoc everywhere:

In the early '90s, East Asian countries had liberalized their financial and capital markets—not because they needed to attract more funds (savings rates were already 30 percent or more) but because of interna-tional pressure, including some from the U.S. Trea-sury Department. These changes provoked a flood of short-term capital—that is, the kind of capital that looks for the highest return in the next day, week, or month, as opposed to long-term investment in things like factories. In Thailand, this short-term capital helped fuel an unsustainable real estate boom. And, as people around the world (including Americans) have painfully learned, every real estate bubble eventually bursts, often with disastrous consequences. Just as suddenly as capital flowed in, it flowed out. And, when everybody tries to pull their money out at the same time, it causes an economic problem. A big economic problem.

When the Thai economy collapsed, the International Monetary Fund, as if working according to a long-prepared plan, began to impose on Thailand the severest austerity measures. The crisis spread to other East Asian nations according to the very same pattern of events, and "even as evidence of the policy's failure mounted—the IMF barely blinked, delivering the same medicine to each ailing nation that showed up on its doorstep."

Stiglitz was convinced, he says, that in such circumstances austerity measures would prove to be very harmful—and so they did. High interest rates have tremendously burdened the already highly indebted East Asian firms, causing a growing number of bankruptcies and defaults. Stiglitz warned that reduced government expenditures would only shrink the economy further; this indeed took place as he predicted.

One does not have to be a conspiracy theorist in order to understand that there is a very clear logic behind the apparent madness of such policies. We will skip over the details of how Stiglitz tried to lobby for a change in policy and in the IMF bureaucracy and utterly failed. It will be enough to comment that the experts' reactions were diametrically contrary to the letter and spirit of the textbooks of the same economic schools that they themselves had attended (or, in some cases, the books they had written themselves and were teaching from). Even if Stiglitz doesn't explicitly suggest it, we are inclined to assume that he is well aware that a thoroughly thought-out policy is at work here, one that does not represent mere accidents and "mistakes." How could one explain as just another mistake that which has the most dire consequences and yet is repeated over and over again?

> It was maddening. . . . Of course, everybody at the IMF assured me they would be flexible: if their policies really turned out to be overly contractionary, forcing the East Asian economies into deeper recession than necessary, then they would reverse them. This sent shudders down my spine. One of the first lessons economists teach their graduate students is the importance of lags: it takes 12 to 18 months before a change in monetary policy (raising or lowering interest rates) shows its full effects. When I worked in the White House as chairman of the Council of Economic Advisers, we focused all our energy on forecasting where the economy would be in the future, so we could know what policies to recommend today. To play catch-up was the height of folly. And that was precisely what the IMF officials were proposing to do.

We will spare the reader detailed description of the no less shattering policies and highly questionable methods that the IMF has adopted to achieve its aims in developing countries. Stiglitz feels compelled to mention in this connection that the

IMF experts labor in that infamous tradition in which, since the end of the nineteenth century, well-meaning Anglo-American imperialists have felt that they are "shouldering Rudyard Kipling's white man's burden." However, Stiglitz insists, this approach is not very helpful if you wish to truly serve the needs of others:

> IMF experts believe they are brighter, more educated, and less politically motivated than the economists in the countries they visit. In fact, the economic leaders from those countries are pretty good—in many cases brighter or better educated than the IMF staff, which frequently consists of third-rank students from first-rate universities. (Trust me: I've taught at Oxford University, MIT, Stanford University, Yale University, and Princeton University, and the IMF almost never succeeded in recruiting any of the best students.) Last summer, I gave a seminar in China on competition policy in telecommunications. At least three Chinese economists in the audience asked questions as sophisticated as the best minds in the West would have asked.

The remarkable point here is that, in the name of western expertise and know-how, precisely the reverse of what was written in the textbooks studied in American universities was practiced in the developing world. Stiglitz, we should note, has been one of the leading theoreticians and teachers in his capacity as a professor of economics at Stanford University over the last 30 years. He writes that the IMF "claimed that all it was asking of the East Asian countries was that they balance their budgets at a time of recession." But what could be the motivating economic logic behind this demand? Stiglitz must have felt that an hour of truth had come in order to broach this subject as he did, unmasking the doublespeak that is so common in western political and economic circles and that encourages one to demand from others the very opposite of what one practices in one's own nation.

Stiglitz mentions that just when the IMF was making this "request" of the East Asian countries, the Clinton administration had just fought a major battle with Congress to stave off a balanced-budget amendment in this country. "Wasn't the administration's key argument that, in the face of recession, a little deficit spending might be necessary?" Stiglitz asks, adding, "This is what I and most other economists had been teaching our graduate students for 60 years. Quite frankly, a student who turned in the IMF's answer to the test question 'What should be the fiscal stance of Thailand, facing an economic downturn?' would have gotten an F."

With the spread of the crisis in Indonesia in late 1997, Stiglitz suggested at a meeting of finance ministers and central-bank governors in Kuala Lumpur "a carefully prepared statement vetted by the World Bank," to the effect that the same austerity and contractionary monetary and fiscal policies that had brought about such havoc in Thailand would create even worse turmoil in Indonesia. However, as in the past, IMF leadership refused to listen to any advice. "The fund's managing director, Michel Camdessus, said there what he'd said in public: that East Asia simply had to grit it out." The IMF pressed ahead and demanded further and more radical reductions in government spending. "And so subsidies for basic necessities like food and fuel were eliminated at the very time when contractionary policies made those subsidies more desperately needed than ever." The crisis deepened, consistently and mercilessly fueled by the selfsame measures. The "domino effect" collapse of the East Asian economic success could no longer be avoided.

By January 1998, output in some of the affected countries had fallen 16 percent or more. Half the businesses in Indonesia were in virtual bankruptcy or close to it and, as a result, the country could not even take advantage of the export opportunities the lower exchange rates provided. Unemployment soared, increasing as much as tenfold, and real wages plummeted—in countries with basically no safety nets. Not only was the IMF not restoring economic confidence in East Asia, it was undermining the region's social fabric. And then, in the spring and summer of 1998, the crisis spread beyond East Asia to the most explosive country of all—Russia.

Stiglitz maintains that the calamity in Russia "shared key characteristics with the calamity in East Asia—not least among them the role that IMF and U.S. Treasury policies played in abetting it. But, in Russia, the abetting began much earlier." He goes on to describe how, following the fall of the Berlin Wall, American policy toward Russia was controlled by those economists who "had little knowledge of the history or details of the Russian economy and didn't believe they needed any."

President Yeltsin's economic policy left Russia's economic assets prey to the scandalous and highly corrupt "loan for shares" national looting program formulated by Yeltsin acolytes Anatoly Chubais and former Russian prime minister Yegor Gaidar, with the close supervision and support of U.S. Treasury Secretary Summers and the IMF. Under the high-level political umbrella of the special U.S.-Russia committee established by Al Gore and another former Russian prime minister, Victor Chernomyrdin, the "Harvard boys," as Gaidar and Chubais were later to be called, led by Harvard economist

Jeffrey Sachs (who later strongly regretted his role), became fanatics for the "universal truth" that "shock therapy works for countries in transition to a market economy: the stronger the medicine (and the more painful the reaction), the quicker the recovery."

Stiglitz reveals that the Treasury Department and the IMF were successful in making it impossible for any open debate on their policies and so could enjoy a free hand before the details of the immense damage done to Russia became known. "Those who opposed this course were either not consulted or not consulted for long." Stiglitz recounts that "on the Council of Economic Advisers . . . for example, there was a brilliant economist, Peter Orszag, who had served as a close adviser to the Russian government and had worked with many of the young economists who eventually assumed positions of influence there. He was just the sort of person whose expertise the Treasury and the IMF needed. Yet, perhaps because he knew too much, they almost never consulted him."

And as Stiglitz describes, we know what came next for Russia:

> The rapid privatization urged upon Moscow by the IMF and the Treasury Department had allowed a small group of oligarchs to gain control of state assets. . . . [T]he IMF and Treasury had laid the groundwork for the oligarchs' plundering. While the government lacked the money to pay pensioners, the oligarchs were sending money obtained by stripping assets and selling the country's precious national resources into Cypriot and Swiss bank accounts. . . . The United States was implicated in these awful developments. In mid-1998, Larry Summers, soon to

be named Robert Rubin's successor as Secretary of the Treasury, actually made a public display of appearing with Anatoly Chubais, the chief architect of Russia's privatization. In so doing, the United States seemed to be aligning itself with the very forces impoverishing the Russian people. No wonder anti-Americanism spread like wildfire.

Through the mid-1990s, the situation became much worse for Russia. With the looting of Russia's real economic assets, the economic output plummeted by half. "While only two percent of the population had lived in poverty even at the end of the dismal Soviet period, 'reform' saw poverty rates soar to almost 50 percent, with more than half of Russia's children living below the poverty line." Nowadays, Stiglitz writes, Russia is "beset by enormous inequality, and most Russians, embittered by experience, have lost confidence in the free market. . . ."

According to Stiglitz, bad economics are only a symptom of the real problem, which is the deeply undemocratic nature of the international, but actually American-dominated, monetary, fiscal, and trade system. He believes that the combination of secrecy and arrogance created a wholly opaque and nontransparent system, and, "more frightening, even internal critics, particularly those with direct democratic accountability, were kept in the dark. The Treasury Department is so arrogant about its economic analyses and prescriptions that it often keeps tight—much too tight—control over what even the President sees."

Stiglitz's last words are worth quoting in full:

Since the end of the cold war, tremendous power has flowed to the people entrusted to bring the gospel of the market to the far corners of the globe. These economists, bureaucrats, and officials act in the name of the United States and the other advanced industrial countries, and yet they speak a language that few average citizens understand and that few policymakers bother to translate. Economic policy is today perhaps the most important part of America's interaction with the rest of the world. And yet the culture of international economic policy in the world's most powerful democracy is not democratic.

This is what the demonstrators shouting outside the IMF next week will try to say. Of course, the streets are not the best place to discuss these highly complex issues. Some of the protesters are no more interested in open debate than the officials at the IMF are. And not everything the protesters say will be right. But, if the people we entrust to manage the global economy—in the IMF and in the Treasury Department—don't begin a dialogue and take their criticisms to heart, things will continue to go very, very wrong. I've seen it happen.

Notes
1. Joseph Stiglitz is professor of economics at Stanford University and at Columbia University, and a senior fellow at the Brookings Institution. From 1997 to 2000, he was chief economist and vice president of the World Bank. He served on the President's Council of Economic Advisers from 1993 to 1997.

Chapter 8

℣

The 77 Group Meeting at Havana

IN THE SAME WEEK IN WHICH THE WORLD BANK AND IMF WERE
holding their meeting in Washington, D.C. (April 14–17,
2000), strongly pressed by the demonstrators and criticized by
congressional committees and representatives, Stiglitz, and
other mainstream economists, a much less publicized event,
though certainly not less significant, was taking place in
Havana, Cuba.

Addressing at least 40 heads of state at a summit meeting
of the 77 Group (formed in 1964 by 77 developing nations,
but now comprising 132 nations), Fidel Castro called for the
elimination of the International Monetary Fund, accusing it of
spreading world poverty, and claiming that "the images we see
of mothers and children in whole regions of Africa under the
lash of drought and other catastrophes remind us of the
concentration camps of Nazi Germany." However, he
continued, "We lack a Nuremberg to judge the economic order
imposed upon us, where every three years more men, women,
and children die of hunger and preventable diseases than died
in the Second World War." President Olusegun Obasanjo of
Nigeria stated, "Never has the world witnessed such massive
disparities in international social and economic activities." The
emerging global gap between the rich and the poor, he said,
constitutes "a major threat to international peace and secu-

rity." Prime Minister Mahathir Mohamad of Malaysia described the global economic system that allowed "rogue currency traders" to destroy the social and economic infrastructure of whole Asian nations built in decades of hard and prosperous labor: "Millions were thrown out of work and made destitute; the international economic institutions moved in ostensibly to help with loans but in reality to facilitate the takeover of the country's economy and even politics."[1]

Together, the 132 developing nations of the 77 Group represent 80 percent of the world's population. The point, I believe, is not whether we agree or disagree with specific formulations from this or that side. The main question is: Are we listening at all seriously to what 80 percent of the world is telling the other 20 percent? Some will feel compelled to reject such views as those put forward by Castro as "extremist" and biased against the "West." It may or not be so; however, we may miss the main issue altogether if we forget that—whether we like it or not—a great majority of human beings today, our sisters and brothers who live with us on a small and densely populated planet, *do* feel that way.

As the 77 Group was meeting in Cuba, another key leader from Africa, the otherwise very careful and reserved Nelson Mandela, was visiting Britain for the first time since retiring as president of South Africa. In an interview with the London *Guardian*, Mandela spoke unequivocally concerning the dangerous power gap that exists today between the leading Anglo-American nations and the rest of the world ("the West versus the rest," to borrow the outrageous expression coined by the leading American political scientist Samuel Huntington):

Tony Blair is a young man I like very much. But I am resentful about the type of thing that America and

Britain are doing. They want now to be the policemen of the world and I'm sorry that Britain has joined the U.S. in this regard.

Referring to bilateral Anglo-American and NATO actions in Iraq and Yugoslavia that ignored the United Nations and the international agreements on states' sovereignty, Mandela commented that: "It's a totally wrong attitude. . . . They must persuade those countries like China or Russia who threaten to veto their decisions at the U.N. They must sit down and talk to them. They cannot just ignore and start their own actions." The leaders of industrialized nations should have listened—should still listen—to such voices from the "third world," because the global social and political balance at the beginning of the twenty-first century is incredibly unstable. What we urgently need today is precisely the reverse of what American and western European leaders are doing. What we need today is to develop the shared human feeling that, on our small and compact globe, power politics of the old kind is already—and is going to be—inherently suicidal for humanity. The world wars of the last century were basically European or northern hemispheric events. If the same power struggle and the same "great games" played by the British and now the American global "sole super-power" engulf the whole planet, then the world wars of the future will be much more disastrous than the two great European-centered wars of the twentieth century.

Notes
1. *New York Times*, April 13, 2000.

Chapter 9

❦

The Moral Divide

WHILE AT THE END OF THE NINETEENTH CENTURY, AND, unfortunately, for much of the twentieth century, materialistic and positivist world views figured as mainstream foundations of all major social ideologies—left, right, and center—this is no longer the case today. Only very few insightful people saw 100 years ago that the present materialistic worldview is as short-sighted as it is culturally and socially destructive. Humanity learned to witness materialism's consequences in reality, and not as theory or ideology, through the horrors of its manifestation as materialistic communism, fascism, national socialism, and capitalism. Will globalization continue in the same direction, or shall we find the new forces needed to transform it towards human ends?

Globalization's central question is: Is the essence of reality, the universe, and the human accidental, non-intelligent, non-benevolent chance, or does spirit exist and create matter, life, and consciousness in the first, middle, and last place? Is the human an emergent, creative agent in a vastly creative and intelligent, holistic universe—part of an immense and awe-inspiring co-creation process, in which the smallest earthly deeds and social conditions have central significance—or are human values, ideas, cultural, and moral creations dust- and death-born, and dust- and death-bound? The answer to this perennial question can be translated, as never before, immedi-ately contrary to today's economic, political, and cultural social strategies and policies.

The divide between the new form of Roman imperial mate-rialism and the new forms of spiritualized economy, polity, and culture, will increasingly constitute the social and anti-social life conditions and formations of humanity in the twenty-first century. As we learn more about the disastrous social effects of this divide the world over, we see that it becomes more acute the more the project of elite globalization advances. The fruits of individuation, which are physical, social, and cultural wealth and prosperity, are now divided according to opposite world conceptions and practices. The classic and neo-Darwinian/Malthusian theories illustrated above represent a continuation and adaptation of older elite approaches to the question of the meaning of human life and the best way to form societies—approaches that are as old as Asian and Egyptian priestly totalitarianism and Roman imperial czarism. The infa-mous elite conception of the 80 to 20 ratio is such a conception. It is basically an egoistical, scarcity-based, social-pyramidal control model, founded on the arguably wholly unscientific belief that natural resources are limited, human resources are finite, and therefore human evolution can only be guaranteed if most of the resources are secured for as few people as possible.

The "fittest" thus "survive" while keeping the majority in the greatest possible ignorance and social-cultural poverty. Corporate consumerism is admirably suited for the purpose; the elites, protected behind the fences of guarded suburbia, use the money they make selling junk to the masses to consume the fruits of classical culture, education, and the arts. The increas-ingly unemployed or meaninglessly employed populace are to be entertained through the modern version of the Roman "bread and circuses," which, to use the charming expression of Brzezinski, has been called "tittytainment"—that is, the keeping of the masses in an infantile state of sucking at the breasts of cheap foods, ever-deteriorating social and cultural services, and a deepening sense of human unworthiness and the meaninglessness of life. This descendant of Roman mass intoxication of the socially and culturally estranged populace through sex, brutality, and fast foods is elite globalization's cultural project for the twenty-first century. It must be as consciously countered by a spiritual and human approach to culture developed by global civil society.

Civil society is now in a position to replace the concept of "elite individuation," which grounds the social-moral code of the elite globalization project. In its place we can create a social reality in which individuation leads to true freedom, and freedom becomes moral-social motivation. Instead of egoistic individuation of the elite, civil society will demonstrate that individual freedom can bring about universal sharing of the social and economic fruits of individuation in order to dramatically increase the global social welfare.

Part II

The Spiritual Origins of Individuation and Threefold Social Differentiation and Integration

THE EMERGENCE OF GLOBAL CIVIL SOCIETY AS A THIRD SOCIAL force—beside the economy and polity—is a recognized fact. It became increasingly so in the 1990s, with the "Earth Summit" in Rio de Janeiro in 1992, through the toppling of the WTO ministerial meeting in Seattle in 1999, to the Johannesburg Summit on sustainable development in 2002. Empirically speaking, it is beyond dispute that, whatever we think about it, civil society is the third sector of an emerging threefold local, national, and global social order. Below, I will show how this development is part of humanity's evolution of consciousness and symptomatic of the next stages of cultural and societal individuation, threefold social differentiation, and integration.

First, I shall argue that tri-sectorialism is inherently linked to recent changes in the evolution of consciousness and constitutes a natural outcome of a certain stage of individuation. Individuation leads to decentralization and differentiation of centralized and hierarchical religious, intellectual, social, and political

formations and functions. It leads to the reintegration of independent social agents and operates in new social processes and
structures. These new social structures emerge the more the
"one center"—whether God, Church, State, Party, Idea, or
Capital—is decentralized. Individualized yet networked, organ-
ically integrated social groups arise, where many centers grow
in flexible, changeable, timely constellations.

Second, I will point out that the potential strength of global
civil society—a strength that distinguishes it markedly from its
predecessors—is found in the fact that this society is much
more conscious of the spiritual and cultural origins of societal
issues. In particular, there is a well-grounded consensus among
many of the leaders of civil society that, to use the phrase
coined by *Tikkun* magazine editor Michael Lerner, "spirit
matters"; that states and stages of mind, heart, and consciousness are changeable and expandable; that evolution of
consciousness is the rule, not the exception, in the universe and
human life. In contradistinction to the determinism of the nineteenth century's views of "the limits of human consciousness,"
the very essence of cognition and consciousness holds the
potential for "trans-formation" and "meta-morphosis." Civil
society itself is a sign that, since the '60s, millions of people the
world over have experienced this. Through many and diverse
spiritual practices, old and new, there have been surprising
developments, mind-expanding discoveries, inventions, and
concepts of modern science and technology. Human encoun-
ters with human destiny, death, birth, illness, and resurrection
have deepened. In all areas of life, creativity, the driving force
of cultural and social transformation in our time, is itself a
dynamically self-transforming enterprise, whose boundaries
have expanded beyond anything that the nineteenth- and early
twentieth-century humans could have imagined.

Chapter 10

Threefolding in Historical Perspective

SOCIOLOGISTS, ANTHROPOLOGISTS, AND HISTORIANS OF modern times are noticing that the evolution of human consciousness is moving to greater stages of individuation. Individuation as conceived below appears to be a most powerful evolutionary driving force behind the human evolution of consciousness, especially since the fifteenth century. Since then, the historical changes brought about in human society—in culture, polity, and economy—are symptoms of this powerful thrust. Individuation breaks down old and collective modes of social organization and cultural-spiritual community and uniformity, and creates new ones, demolishing them in turn when they become hindering forces of centralization in their own right. It thus not only separates the members of any community from each other but, at the same time, diversifies and decentralizes the different social functions. Individuation also changes the individual's state of consciousness and cognition by supporting the development of the faculties of independent judgment and conduct. Hand in hand with the age of discovery and the daring free spirits that founded natural science in the sixteenth and seventeenth centuries, the modern western democratic state emerged, exemplifying a further step of social emancipation by giving individuals a far greater space in which to realize their freedom. The emergence of western European and American cultures from the fifteenth to the nineteenth centuries was based on this phase in the evolution of consciousness, which reached a high point at the end of the nineteenth century and was shattered again by the devastating social upheavals of the twentieth century.

This capacity of individuation—as an expression of the human drive for universal becoming—must be actively and continuously regained at each new stage of development. Our conscious struggle today is to use this capacity and, at the same time, remain universal. As in biological development, the more differentiated an organism, the more integrated it becomes with its milieu. Self-organization, as Humberto Maturana and Francisco Varela demonstrated,[1] is "autopoietic"; that is, inner, genetic differentiation is the organism's answer to the demands of its environment, and its integration into the fabric of reality is an active, self-driven creativity. Today, we must learn to achieve socially what nature achieved through evolution. We have to learn how to achieve a conscious social balance between clear differentiation and cooperative integration of our social faculties and sectors.

A solution to this dilemma is never given and static. It is the revealed secret of evolution itself. This becoming faces in our time, as it did at all times, formidable obstacles. Socially speaking, there are three clearly distinct levels (the economic, the political, and the cultural) at which this struggle is being fought in our own age, at which it is decided whether, and to what extent, human becoming will be fostered, thwarted, or directed towards contrary ends.

In ancient civilizations, notably in the caste system in India, a human being was predestined to occupy a social role, and was bound to this role through inheritance. In his *Republic*, Plato provided another example of a society in which the population is divided according to strict, limited specializations and fixed capacities. In the Middle Ages, too, social standing was inherited and fixed.

Today, each human being seeks to actualize his or her full human nature on all three levels, both individually and in his or her chosen community. On all three, it is human nature—origins and future becoming—that are being contested. Through all three, the "moral divide" of our time, which separates ideas, values, and deeds in the cultural, political, and economic sectors, is operating and deepening.

The realization of the human as an evolving, future-oriented, universally individualized, open, and creative being requires suitable social formations. Since the Renaissance, this necessity has driven successive waves of social, cultural, and religious renewal and change. It was carried further in the powerful impulse that brought reformation of religious experience, ritual, and priesthood in the sixteenth century. It was enhanced yet again in the great scientific and philosophical breakthroughs of the seventeenth century, with the remarkable intellectual and scientific acumen of Johannes Kepler, Galileo Galilei, Sir Isaac Newton, and René Descartes. In the transition to the eighteenth century, this newborn force of the mind was becoming widespread, inspiring confidence in human individuality among the middle classes in Europe. And the fruits of the Renaissance, the Reformation, natural science, and the Enlightenment were gathered, enhanced, and brought to the political level during the American and French revolutions. There, emancipation, individuation, and socialization were expressed by means of the struggle for freedom, equality, and brotherhood.

As Anthony Giddens has shown,[2] the first historical expression of the threefold demand was not a threefold social formation but a centralized one, with the political sector—ideally responsible for equality by means of law and order—taking over most of the functions of the two other sectors. When democracy was secured in America, England, France, and Italy in the course of the nineteenth century, it was the centralized democratic state that was first considered to be the best vehicle for the realization of this threefoldness. A mighty centralized political state took over cultural-spiritual life—where freedom should reign—and the economic life, in which brotherhood and solidarity should have come into existence. Today we know that, so long as one center instead of three autonomous sectors rules, "the center cannot hold; / Mere anarchy is loosed upon the world."[3]

The uniqueness of this threefold conception of society, developed first by Rudolf Steiner at the end of World War I, is that it starts from phenomenological observation of *the whole human being*, and not from ideological principles, philosophical deliberation, or political interests.[4] It views human society as the place in which this human wholeness should find its actualization. Its general anthropological conception of the human includes the whole human being, expressing its basic nature through a dynamic threefold accord, constantly pulsating with differentiation-integration, actualization, and de-actualization processes, whose main sites are characterized as "body, soul, and spirit." In order to achieve fuller self-actualization, human beings in our age increasingly seek to individuate themselves in their bodily life (economic sector), soul life (political-rights sector), and spiritual life (cultural-spiritual sector). This means that the justified demands of the American and French revolutions can be realized. We will find needed freedom in the cultural-spiritual sector, in order to develop our individual potentials, talents, and dispositions. We will find the benefit of equality in the political sector because the worth of each human being is equal to the worth of another, and hence must have an equal share in the social "general welfare." And we will practice solidarity and cooperation in the economic sector and be communally engaged—as producer, consumer, and distributor—together with our fellow human beings. We will be able to determine the terms of the market, such as prices and conditions of credit, in human-to-human, social intercourse and rational agreement.

* * *

The nineteenth century ended with remarkable achievements in all fields of human life; this gave substance to the illusion that the twentieth century would have a straight continuation and a linear enhancement of the same. However, nothing could have been further from the truth. We first had to discover, rather painfully, that individuation is dangerous terrain, full of unknowns and hidden turns and abysses. It turned out to be far removed from the nineteenth-century dream of linear, one-dimensional mechanical progress. The transition to the twentieth century required a tremendous quantum leap from one major paradigm to another. Only now, after one hundred years, have we begun to surmise the outlines of the transformation needed. At the time, it was wholly misunderstood. Humanity stood on the threshold of the twentieth century with its eyes shut, tenaciously ignoring the new and unexplored human and cosmic landscapes immediately ahead.

As modern physics, chemistry, biology, and cosmology discovered, complex systems in equilibrium and those in states far from equilibrium go through sudden bifurcations, tremors, and rapid fluctuations when they draw near zones of singularities. These are hidden variables, or "black holes," through which old orders are shattered or annihilated and new ones arise. As if through singularities, higher forces emerge, wreak chaos in a stable state of affairs, and introduce formative forces of another, more complex, dimension. When complex systems approach such a zone of instability and transformation, a "phase transition"—a leap from one order to another, from one consistency to the next—may occur spontaneously. "Self-organized criticality," a term coined by the Danish scientist, Per Bak,[5] captures well this aspect of any threshold crisis, breakthrough, and transformation. In the words of Ilya Prigogine and Isabelle Stengers, "We begin to have a glimpse of the road that leads from being to becoming. . . . The human race is in a period of transition."[6] Creative chaos may constitute a threshold for a qualitative leap in which hidden, un-actualized possibilities differentiate internally, then externally reorganize and reform masses of particles into new patterns. In such cases, particles or cells abruptly change their particular behavior and affiliations as they become integrated into a global, system-wide coherence, and obey the holistic interrelationships shaped by formative forces operating on a macrocosmic scale. Continuous evolution does make those leaps, and strange, unpredictable, chaotic attractors manifest historical black holes and singularities whenever a major shift is timed at a certain historical threshold. We now realize that everything is constantly changing and evolving not only in nature but also in human history.

This applies also to the formation of modern social life as a whole and, in particular, with regard to the organization of the modern state, the division of power and work among the three sectors. The refusal to understand social evolution as a result of individuation led at the beginning of the twentieth century to the fatal belief in the all-powerful state, in socialism and communism, nationalism and fascism, and as a useful tool in the hands of capitalists. To the same extent that the natural sciences were forced to transform themselves in radical ways between the end of the nineteenth century and the start of the twentieth, so should our economic, political, and cultural structures have been transformed.

At the end of the nineteenth century, European-centered enthusiasm regarding the truly admirable achievements of natural science and technology led to the development of the grand materialistic metaphysics that drove European civilization to its downfall. Political theorist Karl Marx, evolutionists T. H. Huxley and Ernst Häckel, physiologists Jacob Moleschott and Emil Du Bois–Reymond, philosopher Ludwig Büchner, and psychoanalyst Sigmund Freud carried on the waves of this enthusiasm. They helped natural and human sciences to complete materialistic belief systems and worldviews that described the universe, nature, and the human in mechanical, biologically, and psychologically reductionist ways.

Nevertheless, modern research was emerging—in electricity and electromagnetism, the atom, and soon relativistic and quantum physics—that radically undermined those materialistic metaphysics. Here we can notice clear parallels that exist between the evolution of human consciousness as exemplified in the development of the sciences, and that as exemplified in social and political development. As materialism was becoming a new, fundamental religion of the West, the state was enshrined as the new personified social God. The semireligious belief in the all-powerful centralized state on the political left, middle, and right was at its most delirious heights precisely at the moment when the centralized state had to be transformed into a new, threefold social formation. This was the moment when humanity was plunging into the tremendous social earthquakes and revolutions of World War I and the rise of bolshevism, fascism, National Socialism, and Anglo-American domination of the planet. The twentieth century became the century of world wars fought between centralized states, administered by cog-like accomplices, that realized anti-human policies, using their vast economic, political, and cultural power to perpetrate radical evil throughout the world.

In the course of development and evolution, older, crystallized forms may for a time obscure and threaten the emergence of the new, young shoots of the future. But new things *must* come to pass in one way or another when their time is due. Individuation cannot be stopped, only distorted, repressed, and caricatured. But it will always come again as the next challenge. Therefore, the more entrenched the refusal to acknowledge them, and the harder the ground they have to break through in order to grow, the more catastrophic will be the social upheaval, chaos, and destruction. In addition, the true nature and forms of the new impulses will be distorted and kept obscure for long time to come. As historian Niall Ferguson indicates, if we study the beginning of the twentieth century looking backward, we will see that it could well have taken a very different path.[6] Far more rational economic, political, and cultural-spiritual options for action were available, and, once realized, could have saved humanity two world wars, entirely changing the twentieth century.

At the time when humanity was ready to outgrow political centralization, the western state was still centralized around the political core that prevails over both practical economics and cultural affairs. At the threshold that would decide and define human history for centuries to come, human consciousness reeled back in fear. The failure of the leading classes—particularly of the middle class, the intellectuals, academicians, and industrialists, not to mention politicians, in all western, middle, and east European countries—was overwhelming in its totality. Humanity could have assumed a much greater stage of maturity in these countries—asking for decentralized and flexible social structures in which the individual could assume direct responsibility for the economic, political, and cultural life of his or her community and society.

The next step in individuation, which decentralizes the state into mutually supporting, differentiated-integrated autonomous social agents and sectors, has long been due. It will allow individuation to reach the next level of realization, in which each person is free to participate directly in the economic, political-democratic, and cultural-spiritual sectors according to his or her needs and abilities. Individuation becomes at this stage a fully creative and socially formative force. As in the past, it served to demolish the old, hierarchical, centralized, social and cultural medieval theocratic pyramids, and brought about the great revolution of modern democracy, it is now ripe to deepen the democratic state itself, moving it to its next level of social formation.

Notes

1. Humberto R. Maturana and Francisco J. Varela, *Autopoiesis and Cognition: The Realization of the Living* (Boston Studies in the Philosophy of Science, V. 42), Dordrecht, Holland: D Reidel Pub Co; 1991.
2. See Anthony Giddens, *Runaway World: How Globalization Is Reshaping Our Lives* (London and New York: Routledge, 2002) and *Modernity and Self Identity: Self and Society in the Late Modern Age* (Oxford: Blackwell Publishers, 1991).
3. W. B. Yeats, "The Second Coming," 1921. *The Collected Poems of W. B. Yeats* edited by Richard J. Finneran (New York: Scribner, 1996).

4. Rudolf Steiner, *Social Issues: Meditative Thinking and the Threefold Social Order*, translated by Joe Reuter and Sabine H. Seiler (Great Barrington, MA: Anthroposophic Press, 1996).
5. See *How Nature Works: The Science of Self-Organized Criticality* (Copernicus, N.Y. & Oxford: Oxford University Press, 1997).
6. Ilya Prigogine and Isabelle Stengers, *Order Out of Chaos: Man's New Dialogue with Nature* (New York: Bantam, 1984).
7. "And one of the alternative outcomes of the First World War is that Britain stays neutral. And therefore you have a continental rather than a world war...[I]t's clear that the Germany of 1914, had it been successful in its objective of defeating its continental neighbors, would have created something not unlike the European Union. . . .The Third Reich could never have come about without the defeat of 1918, and all the subsequent upheavals. . . [I]f the war had been won [Hitler] would have been a contented second-rate artist with nothing to complain about. . . ." (Niall Ferguson in an interview with Bill Goldstein, *The New York Times*, April 20, 1999.)

Chapter 11

☙

The Weakening of the Modern State: Global Economy Rules the World

THE MAJOR POWER THAT DESTABILIZES THE MODERN STATE IS the modern economy. Economic globalization is tearing away from the state most of its economic, political, and cultural assets, and, as long as no strong threefold alternative is provided, the forces of the elite globalization project will increasingly transfer public assets and services into private corporate and financial hands. Only a clear understanding and practical implementation of threefold social interactions and relationships among the three sectors of society will check the powers that be and replace the centralized state with more adequate modern social forms.

To avoid misunderstanding, a distinction must be made between the critique of globalization offered here and the wholesale rejection of globalization. Our point is that in economic and technological terms, globalization does represent a timely and valuable advance for human civilization. However, the social challenge is to learn how to use its benefits for the *greater good of humanity as a whole*. It is here that differences exist, as that term itself has always been given the most diverse and contrary interpretations.

It is important not to juxtapose the increasingly global production, consumption, and exchange of goods, services, and information (which *could* lead to greater universal welfare) with the misuse of the same powers that comes about when individuals, corporations, institutions, and states use the same developments in order to increase the welfare of only a small part of humanity instead of the whole. Globalization also represents a welcome advance in creative human innovation in many fields of science and technology. How these innovations are used is a matter of social and cultural values; their misuse has nothing to do with science as such, but with human interests. It is the continued subordination of economics, human rights, and cultural values to one-sided and shortsighted interests that is designated here by the term "elite globalization."

As many studies demonstrate, at least one paramount cause for the almost unlimited power of elite globalization's values and interests over broader economic, environmental, human and cultural concerns lies, undoubtedly, with the weakening of equity, law, and human rights in the middle sector, where the democratic state has maintained, and should increase, its justified role. The state, with its governing and legislative apparatuses, should represent the equality of human beings. It should be the middle ground that adjusts and harmonizes the demands of the markets and the cultural values of its citizens. This is the basis for the democratic process—the equality of all citizens based on the recognition that they, as sovereign individuals, are to determine together with their peers the rules that apply equitably to all mature citizens in the social community of their state.

The democratic process is founded on the self-conscious experience of freedom and on the experience of equality, as free individuals know that they are equal to each other in worth. Only free people can recognize the equal value of other humans, because only they can recognize their own human value in relation to others. Thus democracy receives (and must constantly receive) its legitimacy from individual consciousness of freedom. Modern democracy is based on a remarkable cultural and spiritual breakthrough that takes place in the self-consciousness of sovereign individuals. It receives its legitimacy when free humans begin to practice their feelings and intuitions concerning human equity and human rights, and to give them social form. The democratic institutions of the political state, which provide laws and security, guarantee human rights, and protect citizens' cultural values, constitute some of these forms.

Without the ability to engage the citizens of a state, region, or community in an ongoing social process that clarifies continually what the human rights, wrongs, and values in that community's time and place are, other, less human interests will always have the upper hand. It is therefore not so difficult to realize that the subjugation of the second sector to one-sided, anti-human, unaccountable global markets, business and financial forces is one of the immanent causes of many of the worst social wrongs brought about by elite globalization:

> The most disturbing aspect of this global system is that the formidable power and mobility of global corporations are undermining the effectiveness of national governments to carry out essential policies on behalf of their people. Leaders of nation-states are losing much of the control over their own territory they once had. . . . Tax laws intended for another age, traditional ways to control capital flows and

interest rates, full employment policies, and old approaches to resource development and environmental protection are becoming obsolete, unenforceable, or irrelevant.[1]

No serious and objective study of globalization will dispute such views today, and a multitude of serious studies and publications have corroborated them in great detail. While I fully endorse these findings, I would like to suggest another perspective for an overall judgment concerning their final social significance. Such a perspective, I believe, can not only accommodate a fully justified critique of elite globalization, but also point to alternative ways of dealing with it. Many critics of globalization focus their attention solely on the weakening of state power and the ways in which state control is taken over by business. Are we not forgetting today, because of our justified concerns with the onslaught of elite globalization, that traditionally the same state whose weakness we now deplore wielded *too much* power, and precisely in areas in which its legitimacy was always justly disputed? Obviously, these are theoretically rather complex questions, and I don't intend to discuss them here. However, the fact that "traditional ways" to control capital, production, and economic planning are becoming impractical may also indicate a need for new and creative social formations, such as the threefold decentralization and integration of the social forces discussed here. Such an approach will find not only the destructive results of the crisis brought about by globalization, but also timely and creative social opportunities, calling for social formations that can address new realities. And globalization is a reality that is not going to disappear. As we shall see below, the once all-powerful state, and the now all-powerful businesses, are increasingly learning that new social formations are emerging by means of which both sectors will learn to share responsibility in a collaborative, *tri-sectoral* way, together with the emerging forces of civil society.

If we do not share this perspective we will have to conclude, in the words of Barnet and Cavanaugh:

> But no political ideology or economic theory has as yet evolved to take account of the tectonic shift that has occurred. . . . [T]he nation state everywhere faces a crisis of redefinition without a practical ideology that confronts the realities of the emerging global order. . . . [A]s national economies become increasingly intertwined, nations are breaking up in many different ways, and no alternative community is yet on the horizon.[2]

Our contention, however, is that Barnet and Cavanaugh are right if they refer to the fact that no new widely accepted political *ideology* or economic *theory* has arisen, but are wrong if they do not notice that an "alternative community" is, as a matter of social-historical fact, already emerging. If this is correct, it means that our political-social and economic models and theories lag, as they often did in the last century, behind new and significant social evolution occurring before our very eyes in real social time.

It is understandable that the second sector—the political state as protector of human rights and equality before the law—is becoming increasingly helpless in the face of global economic pressure. And if this is indeed the case, where should we be looking for new social forces? Where is the social place in which new moral forces can emerge? When we say that we want to strengthen the state, what do we really mean? Do we want to go back to more centralization of the economy and culture in the hands of governments and bureaucracies? Is this the "new" direction? Or, alternatively, are we to search the sphere of human consciousness, responsibility, and freedom in which new social realities are created because individual human beings are free to take social initiatives without dependency on organized market and state forces? Are we to try this alternative—or are we too tired, disillusioned, and skeptical, even cynical, concerning human ability to exercise moral freedom, free choice, and action? If we haven't yet given up the human project, let us now consider the emergent power of the third actor that has recently entered global social affairs and already has shown considerable power to shape economic, political, and cultural change.

Notes

1. Richard J. Barnet and John Cavanaugh, *Global Dreams: Imperial Corporations and the New World Order* (New York: Simon & Schuster, 1994), p. 19.
2. Ibid.

Chapter 12

☙

The Modern State and Centralized Social Structure

WHY WAS THE MODERN STATE AN IMPORTANT STEP TOWARD freedom? Because it broke some of the older, universalistic-monolithic forms of medieval social structure. In each step along the road toward personal and social individuation, expressed in an increasingly decentralized cultural and social milieu, the established organizations, be they cultural, political, or economic, feel as if they are losing the ground under their feet. This was certainly the case at the beginning of the era when the emerging nation state, the mother of modern western democracy, was replacing the monarchical-theocratic social structures of the Middle Ages; and it is also true today as a threefold social formation replaces the centralized democratic state.

The modern state is only a step toward social individuation. From the new point of view of decentralized, tri-sectoral social formations, it is as centralized as if, from its own revolutionary point of view, it looked back at the universal monarchies of the Middle Ages. This modern state owes the old universal monarchy more than it was ready to accept until now. It is strongly conditioned by the traditional, centralized, and hierarchical religious, cultural, economic, military, and social organizational paradigm as it evolved in Europe over the last 1,000 years. This paradigm is essentially a result of the once fruitful—but for today rather unholy—marriage between Catholic Christianity and the politics of the Roman Empire. These religious and political systems merged together in the spiritual and the secular structures of the Middle Ages. On the one hand we have the Roman Catholic church organization, beginning with a totalitarian God at the top of the pyramid, commanding a subordinated celestial hierarchy, copied in the ecclesiastical hierarchy of pope, cardinals, bishops etc. The same system was adopted in the secular Holy Roman Empire of the German nation that ruled middle Europe from the moment of its inauguration by Charles IV's Golden Bull of 1356, until Napoleon dismantled it in 1806.

For western Europe, the emergence and consolidation of the modern nation state took place gradually after the so-called Peace of Westphalia in 1648 (which ended the Thirty Years War) and assumed its present democratic form a century and a half later in the American and French revolutions. However, for many eastern European, Asian, and African countries this emancipatory social process is happening right now in very different social and cultural conditions. The statehood they develop and struggle to maintain must be understood in this evolutionary, relative sense (in the historical "perspectivistic" and flexible—and hence truly diverse and human—manner, as Nietzsche would have it, trying to counter the mechanical deterministic historicism of the late nineteenth century). Only in this way can we stop the continued absurd practice—an intellectual child of positivistic historicist fallacy—that fires the highly inflammable missionary zeal of so many globalizers as they forcefully impose specific and relative western European values, such as "western liberal democracy" and "free market economy," as absolute social commandments on the most diverse countries and cultures around the globe. Quite apart from the fact that this form of centralized democratic western society is itself in a state of dynamic flux and development, and that a shortsighted snapshot of its present evolutionary stage should not be made into an absolute, eternal social gospel, it is often forgotten that similar social transformations in the West took some hundreds of years to reach their present forms. The time required for the ripening of social transformation must not be taken from the newly emerging nation states and democracies. Moreover, they must be allowed to do it in their unique way, as the West did it in its way over the past 500 years. They surely will find their unique social ways—the ways that are healthiest for them—to realize their own social and cultural tasks. And the democratic industrialized nations should be wise enough to offer the help that is truly needed, and not follow the direction of the global expansionism and profiteering of the biggest and most insatiable power-seeking egos.

The treaty of Westphalia recognized the sovereign right of western European nations to form their own united economic, political, and cultural social formations, whose borders would be more or less identical with their national entity. These western nation states not only became the main arbiter for political and legislative matters, but also have assumed responsibility for controlling the economic and cultural-spiritual development and interests of their people. Nobody seriously denies today that tremendous social advancement was achieved in all areas of human society and culture under the protection of the state. The democratic nation state not only regulated human rights and legislation, but also provided law and order, delivered by democratically elected parliaments, governments, and presidents. The state provided for public development and ownership of the means of production;

protection of the economic interests of its producers and traders; and economic planning of production, business, investment, and control and regulation of the influx and exchange rate of national currency. At the same time, the state took over the spheres of cultural life from the ruling elites, providing public education, social, and medical care, and insurance. It administered justice and fostered the national values, ethos and goals of its people. The state became everything economic, political, and cultural, all in and through one and the same centralized, democratic apparatus.

Statehood in this modern sense is, therefore, a wholly necessary evolutionary step, up to a certain point, beyond which it has served its purpose and must make way for the next, more timely evolutionary step. Above, we pointed out that the next step should continue the first and allow for greater individual emancipation, social integration, and participation. This takes the form of threefolding or tri-sectoral partnerships and networks. This will be the next social step for modern democracy as it evolves further to make space for direct participation and creative responsibility—not only in the formal democratic elective process, but also by offering a social arena in which free cultural and economic participation will become as natural for individuals as the democratic. It is a positive step toward individuation of the single person in and through his or her community, because it creates a social space in which collective forms—theocratic, monarchic, religious, ideological, and democratic—are replaced by a social order that is freer and hence more directly democratic. The existing western democracy, be it of the parliamentary British model or the later French and American republicanism, is not a perfect end product of social evolution, but rather one open-ended stage along future paths of individuation and integration.

Thus the modern state—the embodiment of an essential stage of emancipation in comparison to social life in the Middle Ages—is obsolete when looked at from the perspective of the end of the twentieth century and the beginning of the twenty-first. Did this state achieve all that belongs to social emancipation? Has individuation achieved in it its most developed form? My answer is no. It has taken a first step, the political formal step. It took over the responsibility of shaping culture and economy from the ruling classes, and subjected them to more or less democratic control. For this purpose the responsibility for education, sciences and arts, public health, and justice was taken over by the democratic state, and elected officials became responsible for their administration and regulation. Democratically elected representatives became responsible for administrating and answering the human need for generally affordable education and culture, and for greater social equity and justice. At the same time, the state assumed, to varying degrees in different democracies, at least some control and regulation of practical economic matters. "National economy" came into being, simultaneously with the rise of capitalism, colonialism, and the industrial revolutions, because now the state supported, with its newly established tax revenues, the development of all basic physical infrastructures needed for a modern economy.

Schools, universities, hospitals for the general public, transportation, energy, industrial infrastructure, and, unfortunately, state-sponsored warfare—all was now accomplished by and with the generous help of the state. The state became the active agent in cultural life (education, sciences and arts, health care) and in the economy (not only creating the necessary physical economic infrastructures, but actively engaging in regulation and planning of production and becoming the greatest

owner of the means of production in many states) as well. It
also administered law and order and protected human rights
through its parliamentary legislative work.

Replacing the divinely blessed European universal
monarchy, the state became everything political, economic,
and cultural, and the social question as such was now largely
centralized in and through the organization of the democratic
state. This was a vital, positive step forward in human social
emancipation. Through the state, individuation achieved a
major breakthrough, moving toward greater freedom to determine the content of cultural life, to express the newly acquired
recognition of human equality through democratic legislation,
and to regulate, through elected members of the community,
production, consumption, and trade. The republican ideal of
the state as the true guarantor and protector of the "general
welfare"—most beautifully expressed in the U.S. Constitution—was realized, at least to a certain degree, for a certain
time, and in certain countries. But it *was* realized.

In living social development, the moment a stage is realized
and felt to be perfect or complete, we are prompted to move
still further. There is nothing eternal in our social life;
"becoming" should have become the buzzword long ago. We
are moving ahead with increasing speed; society is changing
and transforming itself not only from decade to decade but
from year to year. So, as we began to feel that with the modern
state a certain "permanent" solution to the social question had
been accomplished, at that very moment we had to begin and
move ahead again. The time to move courageously ahead was
marked very clearly at the beginning of the twentieth century,
and our inertia and incapacity to do so was demonstrated in
the course of the whole last century: in two terrible world wars

and the Cold War, as well as in the resulting precariously unbalanced global social situation described above.

Clearly, we missed the historical message again and again. Can we do better now?

I maintain that precisely because the democratic revolution was successful, it must press forward with the process of social emancipation, individuation, and free integration. Further major steps are necessary in order to keep the democratic social momentum alive and creative. As the political process was taken over by the community of free, individual human beings and at one time dominated the cultural and economic spheres of life, so now must education, science, the arts and religion—in short, cultural life as a whole—become self-regulatory and emancipated from external coercion and control in order to be administered by the practically involved communities of self-organizing cultural institutions. And in the same way, practical, real, day-to-day economic life must be self-organized by and for free people, who create economic communities, associations, and cooperatives in which consumers come together with producers, traders, and credit givers in order to determine through direct consultations and negotiations how consumer needs will be answered by human-oriented production.

All three social sectors will be increasingly claimed by the individual person. As all citizens have the right, not the obligation, to participate in electing their representatives in the democratic process, based on the equality of each citizen before the law, so true education, artistic creativity, science, and medicine cannot develop under state control or in the so-called "free market" by becoming economic values. They must have freedom as a social base. The state role in this regard is to guarantee, by the decree of legislation, the equality of opportunities, and to allocate the resources needed for the free institutions of the third sector. It must wholly abstain from managing, planning, and practicing in this field. Equality will be maintained by the law, which will guarantee equal rights and equal financial opportunities, on which true freedom in the cultural-spiritual (services) sector will be grounded.

This is the next step in the historical evolution of human consciousness toward greater differentiation, autonomy, and free social integration. Jeffrey Goldstein, in the journal *Emergence*, says that, "In effect, there seems to be no end to the emergence of emergents. Therefore, the unpredictability of emergents will always stay one step ahead of the ground won by prediction. As a result, its seems that emergence is now here to stay."[1] Obviously, this applies to any social initiative and creativity in social life, because any initiative, novelty, or invention is "spiritual" in nature: here freedom must reign, without standardization by the state. We must be able today to have the freedom of openness, flexibility, and renewal that state control never allows. As Uri Merry points out, "Life and social living necessitate systems that can handle constant, small changes within them and around them which never allow them to be the same as before."[2]

This philosophical shift is transforming society. It will change the centralized democratic western state into decentralized and freely integrated threefold—indeed, manifold—social formations, because it will enable the creation of "institutions for freedom," in which emergence, creativity, and the unpredictably new and surprising can be helped into being. The more society develops in this way, the more it will be able to address the challenges of globalization.

Notes

1. Jeffrey Goldstein, "Emergence as a Construct: History and Issues," in *Emergence*, 1(1), 1999, pp. 49–72.
2. Uri Merry, *Coping with Uncertainty: Insights from the New Sciences of Chaos, Self-Organization and Complexity* (Westport, CT: Praeger, 1995), p. 35.

Chapter 13

༄

Civil Society Comes of Age: A Global Call to Conscience

THE TIMELY ANSWER TO THE WEAKENING OF THE CENTRALIZED state by the forces of economic globalization comes from the third social sector—the cultural-spiritual sphere—in which human values, ideas, initiative, and progress are rooted. It is the sphere of global conscience, and the moral force of this conscience became very powerful in the last decades of the twentieth century. A morally autonomous civil society is shaking up and awakening the otherwise state- or market-owned and paralyzed third sector, and reminding artists, scientists, educators, and physicians of their original moral obligations to society. As Nicanor Perlas points out in his book *Shaping Globalization: Civil Society, Cultural Power and Threefolding*, its emergence brings about a *de facto* three-folding of global society. A three-part social dynamism is beginning to replace the old and exhausted bipolar structure that cannot creatively confront the dilemmas presented by economic globalization and environmental, human, and cultural degradation. A tri-sectoral social process is emerging in *reality*, whether we like it or not, and the question is only whether we will be able to support this process in ways that will serve the needs of a greater part of humanity than was hitherto possible under capitalist, social-democratic, and socialist political structures.

This is the main difference between a tri-polar concept of society and the traditional, bi- and uni-polar social-political concepts. However, we see that most critics of globalization, being aware of the above-mentioned recent weakening of the state, when they are challenged to advance from criticism and a stance of opposition to creating positive and innovative social alternatives, come up with no other proposal but—again—stronger state intervention, more or less in the established socialistic and/or social-democratic political traditions of the last hundred years.

The historical paradox is obvious. While most socially active NGOs and individuals are representatives of a newly arising, varied, heterogeneous, and manifold "third sector" of society—that is, an active, free cultural sphere in which "civil society" is rooted—many of them are not yet cognizant of their own new status as an independent third social sector. More often than not, they still look back at the political sector, embodied in the state, as the answer to all difficulties. They lack the concept of social freedom, and of the third sector as the real providers of education, health, and medical services, agriculture, arts, religion, and science. And we have witnessed it again and again—those activists who are eventually elected become part of the bipolar dynamic of economy versus state. More often than not, they realize that they are forced to repeat the same compromises and mistakes as their predecessors, having no new, creative social solutions to the old unresolved dichotomy and struggle between capitalism and socialism.

However, the third sector, or social member, *is* becoming increasingly influential, revealing itself through many NGOs and active individuals the world over, *precisely because* it represents the principle of differentiation, manifoldness, and hence freedom: free civil, social moral/spiritual responsibility makes itself manifest as a new source of social initiative that must be distinguished from state/government and economy/business.

Nicanor Perlas explains how we can find a new conception of the role of civil society, constituting the active and dynamic, morally motivated "spearhead" of the third, cultural-spiritual sector in modern social life:

> First, civil society liberates itself from the clutches of government and corporate control. Civil society creates this space by providing society with independent thinking, advocacy for alternative policies, and criticism and protest of unjust and inequitable government and business practices. Second, by creating this space, civil society activists are thereby irrevocably altering the dynamics of the interactions between the government and business, between civil society and government, and all three simultaneously. . . .
>
> Put in another way, all over the world, civil society has emerged as a powerful countervailing force against the centralizing tendencies in many governments and business institutions advancing elite globalization. Civil society is the potent expression of culture's defense of itself. The beginnings of threefolding occur de facto when civil society manages to protect its space and establish its presence vis-a-vis the two other dominant forces of society, namely government and business.[1]

Sociologists Jean-Louis Cohen and Andrew Arato, in their study of civil society as a third social sector, declare:

> We understand "civil society" as a sphere of social interaction between economy and state, composed above all of the intimate sphere . . ., the sphere of associations . . ., social movements, and forms of public communication. Modern civil society is created through forms of self-constitution and self-mobilization. . . . [T]he superiority of a three-part framework for the understanding of civil society is fundamental for our conception.[2]

This quotation reveals a growing readiness on the part of social science to acknowledge the existence of a "threefold-ness," a trilateral or tri-sectoral "division of labor" within the social body.

There have, of course, been diverse points of view concerning civil society since ancient Greek and Roman times. Our aim here is not to present a historical survey of the concept through the ages, but to indicate some points of departure for gaining a larger perspective on civil society and its role in the current social debate.[3]

Civil society is largely understood as the sphere of human freedom, individual development, and identity, and the cultural values created by means of individual creativity through the ages. One aspect of this is described by Antony Black, a historian of civil society, who writes, "We may identify the central ideal of civil society as personal independence, and its central imperative as respect for persons."[4]

Individualism is in itself a source and ground of a heterogeneous cultural-spiritual community of free spirits. What does the economic sector provide for, after satisfying the physical needs of human life? It provides for education, arts, sciences, health, and well-being, religion, meaning, and values. Individualism is a creator of free, diverse, and multi-cultural community—the cultural community that is society's most vulnerable sector, if we consider the fact that it must rely on the physical means provided by the economic sector—but it is society's most essential foundation insofar as society needs free individual contribution in order to become truly human.

In the history of more ancient forms of civil society, Black says, "Individuation and association went hand in hand. One achieved liberty by belonging to this kind of group. Citizens, merchants and artisans pursued their own individual goals by banding together under oath." Ernest Gellner, in *Conditions of Liberty: Civil Society and Its Rivals,* discovers that it is the place of the individual person that defines the sphere of civil society, and distinguishes this sphere from other spheres of social organization, such as the market or the democratically organized state. Like Cohen and Arato, cited above, Gellner finds that the "modularity of human beings," that is, their social freedom of movement, interaction, association etc., creates the unique social sphere of the "third sector." However, he writes, "In contradistinction to more ancient forms of social aggregates, since modern times the individual has a growing sense and capacity for choosing and hence actually *creating* her or his own social and cultural environments."[5]

The fact that individualism—once considered to be the opposite of community—shared social responsibility and cultural continuation, can actually become a new source of culture, association, common meaning, and values, is revolutionary. Through the making of free economic associations and free cultural and spiritual enterprises, creativity and social responsibility and engagement develop, and a cultural sphere manifests and exists.

In a most comprehensive study to date of NGOs and their social significance, *Constructing World Culture: International Nongovernmental Organizations Since 1875,* John Boli and George Thomas present a comprehensive account of the development of international nongovernmental organizations over the course of more than a century.[6] They examine a range of arenas, from the women's movement to technical standardization, and give an in-depth view of the origins of the third sector, proving that it is a social force that has been emerging gradually during the course of recent history. Most significant is their main conclusion, namely that "international nongovernmental organizations significantly influence other actors in world politics by changing world culture." Their research offers strong empirical and theoretical support to Nicanor Perlas's argument that civil society is a culturally based social phenomenon. Science, technology, entrepreneurship, art, and religion all are rooted in free human consciousness. When our society is based on human nature, and does not work so profoundly against it, we will share the conviction that the management and praxis of education and research, art and medicine, agriculture and environment, must be given to those active in these fields. Autonomy, diversity, self-organization, and creative synergy of multiple, multi-cultural networks will become as self-evident as federal control nowadays.

But this means also, conversely, that culture is not an ivory enclave, an escapist's haven, or a form of more or less refined "entertainment." Shouldn't we be ready to consent to culture's great, central social role? Are the culturally creative people and the forces of human freedom restricted only to creative ideas and discovery (science), art (beauty), and religion (abstract moral precepts and values)? Or should they not be at the same time active and fertile in the most concrete modifications of economic and political developments? And where is the source of economic improvement of the means of production, of trade, transportation, and communications, if not in the human mind? And social intuition of equity and the human feeling for right and wrong embodied in laws: Are they not a free moral creation of the human heart?

Look it up even in such a globalist manifesto as Thomas Friedman's *The Lexus and the Olive Tree*.[7] When he tries to understand the source and influence of values, beliefs, meanings—in short, of "culture"—Friedman must admit that here it is the power of the freely motivated individual that is most significant. He cites the example of one determined person, Jody Williams, who created a vast global movement—forcing 50 governments, in the face of opposition from the hegemonic globalizer Friedman praises so highly, the U.S., to ban landmines—because she responded to the real need of the many people who, ignored by the powerful, are maimed and killed daily all over the world. Her "response-ability" and personal example was the flame that enkindled the latent fire of responsibility in thousands and thousands of other free people, and won her the Nobel Peace Prize in 1997. Even tough globalizers such as Friedman must stand sometimes in awe before such a revelation of human truth. They cannot comprehend the sources of its social authority and power, because they know only two such sources, and can envision no place for a third. They will never concede that this power, which is the source of true culture, is socially equal to economic and political authority. Yet modern civil society finds here its strongest anchor. Over time and at some cost, this power will be heeded even by the most powerful in finance and politics, because its authority is based on the autonomy of the moral imperative that can originate only in individual experience of freedom. The third sector is, therefore, to be understood as the individual and diversified sphere of moral, spiritual, and cultural creativity as such, animating all the values according to which we shape our social relationships and institutions in culture, politics, and the economy. The third sector is the social place where the values and meanings are created that animate society as a whole, and let capital and law be used for the benefit of humanity as a whole.

Notes

1. Nicanor Perlas, *Shaping Globalization: Civil Society, Cultural Power and Threefolding* (Pasig City, Philippines: Center for Alternative Development Initiatives, 2000), Chapter 5, pp. 60–70. In Chapter 6, Perlas elaborates on the matter of civil society as a force rooted in the autonomous moral authority of culture. In Chapter 8, entitled "Civil Society and the Threefolding of National and Global Social Space," he describes civil society as a "de facto self-defense of culture."
2. Jean-Louis Cohen and Andrew Arato, *Civil Society and Political Theory (Studies in Contemporary German Social Thought)* (Cambridge, MA: MIT Press, 1994, reprint edition), pp. ix, 423.
3. For a concise summary of the main social-scientific conceptual developments concerning the nature and role of civil society from Hegel through Gramsci and Parsons to Anthony Giddens, the reader can refer to Chapter 5 in Perlas's book, mentioned above.
4. Antony Black, *Guilds and Civil Society* (Ithaca, NY: Cornell University Press, 1984).
5. Ernest Gellner, *Conditions of Liberty: Civil Society and Its Rivals* (New York: Penguin, 1994).
6. Stanford University Press, 1999.
7. Farrar, Straus, 1999.

Chapter 14

☙

Individuation and Social Decentralization

INDIVIDUATION IS A HISTORICAL AND EVOLUTIONARY PROCESS that unites humanity and makes it, for the first time, a self-conscious social whole, though it exists in differentiated ways and forms around the earth. It leads to a growing experience of subjective freedom and objective cultural diversity that shapes our social life and relationships. It means that each increasingly sovereign individual, group, belief, ethnic community, and national and religious culture wishes to become an independent agent and an active participant in social life in a direct way. No longer at the base of a pyramidal hierarchy by means of which authority in all fields of life—religious, cultural, political, and economic—comes from above, individuals want to be active parents, choosing freely what kind of education is in accordance with their cultural and spiritual values. They want to play an active role in the major decisions concerning the social life of their community or state, according to their understanding of human worth and human rights. They want to be actively engaged in the immediate economic process, either as consumers, producers, or traders, and to take part in determining the prices of the goods produced, exchanged, and consumed.

Individuation as I understand it prompts each individual and community to become active, responsive, and responsible in each of the three main spheres of social life: the sphere of free educational, cultural, and spiritual creativity; the sphere of social equity and human rights; and the sphere of economic solidarity and cooperation. Rather than be subject to a monolithic, even if formally democratic, centralized state, or a monopolistic "free" market, we strive today to be free social and cultural creators, and to create social relationships that will allow individual freedom to express its responsibility where we choose

This was originally felt and expressed, in rather chaotic and sometimes destructive ways, when the first people in Europe and America asked for *freedom, equality, and brotherhood*. Today this sounds like an overly ambitious, farfetched ideal, partly because the efforts to realize them led more often than not to suffering, bloodshed, revolutions, and eventually the very opposite of these ideals: subjugation, inequality, and fratricide. We strive now to begin with more concrete and authentic human experience and down-to-earth definitions of human needs, rather than lofty exclamations of ideals—and properly so, because the way these ideas were conceived, expressed, and practiced reflect the thinking of a much more intellectually inclined age than our own. Nevertheless, the ideas and ideals of a former age become *given natural needs and elemental impulses* in the next. Therefore, it is right that we are speaking today about deep-seated human needs, and include in them all those great and beautiful concepts, those Platonic and classical ideas about beauty, truth, and love, that once seemed to belong to a super-human order of things. Today, these ideas are much more "individualized" than they were in classical times, with the potential to become more, not less, a part of essential human nature.

These social and cultural "ideals" are appearing nowadays as deep-seated psychological and spiritual *needs*; as elementary *requirements* they surface in modern history again and again, in many variations as well as contradictions, but they are rising in each century anew with elemental power. Their origin is not to be found in abstract ideas or ideologies, though after their emergence they may be expressed in this manner. First and foremost, these are essential impulses and human needs, which are as much a part of our *instinctive, emotive, and intuitive* nature as are our so-called "lower" or "animalistic" (whatever that may mean) desires, instincts, and drives. It is, after all, one of the most significant discoveries of modern humanistic psychology that the "spiritual" in the human being is as "instinctive" as the other bodily and soul forces, and that to actualize our "higher" nature (that is, our human creative-spiritual nature) is an instinctive need whose satisfaction or neglect determines human fulfillment to a far greater extent than was thought before, according to the materialistic and reductionist models of human nature. As Stuart Kauffman has taught us, we are indeed "at home in the universe,"[1] because our creativity grew out of the creativity of emergent planetary life, and this life is creative in a human-cosmic sense. Ray Kurzweil says that intelligence is reaching in and through us to galactic heights and expanses, because we are its living embodiment in our universe.[2] Fritjof Capra's "social ecology" is based on such modern scientific insights, maintaining that the human, conceived interactively and holistically, is becoming a self-conscious part of vast, creative, and complex planetary and cosmic webs of beings—that spirit really works from within matter, and that matter is but condensed light of creation.[3] This is a new and timely discovery of the natural and human sciences in the second half of the twentieth century.

The "spiritual"—the human and creative—is not a separate domain in the heavens or a hidden province of the human soul. It is an emergent, becoming, and evolving power, part of the essential creative-emergent nature of the universe in which we are also becoming. It is therefore pushing its way to expression in and through all the levels of our being. The creatively human is a need within need within need, as Theodore Roszak[4] once noted; striving to satisfy our hunger and thirst, our need for comfort and physical and emotional security, we discover the need for truthful, intimate human relations, and as we strive to fill this need we need to come together with our fellow human beings in a just and democratic social and political life.

In order to become creative participants in our democratic society, we discover the values that make it operative; and before too long, behind formal democracy emerges the need for free cultural and spiritual life, the quest for beauty, truth, love, transcendence, and self-transformation, and their realization in daily social life. So this is what humans are made of in the age of individuation in which we live. And, as we have seen above, the longer these higher needs are suppressed, the longer and more severe will be the social upheaval and chaos.

But why is this actually so? Why do so many human beings today feel the need for a direct, personal responsibility in economic, political, and cultural life? Why have we seen, in the last couple of centuries, millions and millions of human beings fight and struggle in order to change social conditions for the better? I do not refer here to the specific agenda of this or that social movement, to this or that theoretical manifesto, be it from the left, right, or middle, but to the fact that millions of ordinary people like us increasingly care, strive to participate, and are hungry to be socially creative. While so many are indifferent and inert, and while others are outright irresponsible, many others care deeply about the local and global social situation of humanity, and ecological, economic, and cultural ideas are experienced, discussed, and acted upon as never before in human history. Where does it all come from?

Notes

1. See Stuart A. Kauffman, *At Home in the Universe: The Search for the Laws of Self-Organization and Complexity* (Oxford: Oxford University Press, 1996).
2. See Ray A. Kurzweil, *The Age of Spiritual Machines: When Computers Exceed Human Intelligence* (New York: Penguin, 2000).
3. See Fritjof Capra, *The Turning Point: Science, Society, and the Rising Culture* (New York: Bantam, 1988).
4. See Theodore Roszak, ed. *Ecopsychology: Restoring the Earth, Healing the Mind* (San Francisco: Sierra Club Books, 1995) and *The Making of a Counterculture: Reflections on the Technocratic Society and Its Youthful Opposition* (Berkeley, CA: U.C. Press, 1995).

Chapter 15

☙

Individuation and Modern Initiation: The Spiritual Origin of Threefolding

ELITE GLOBALIZATION TAKES OVER NATIONAL ECONOMIES, privatizes public infrastructures, and makes schools, hospitals, prisons, research institutions, and social security into tradable, low-quality, and anti-human articles. Today, the West is ruled not by the Catholic church but by a "postmodern" universal monarchy of transnational capital and gigantic corporations. From this power there is only one rescue: the free individual human spirit. As free individuals created the modern state to replace medieval feudal universalism, so today they replace universal elite globalization with threefolding. Individuation, if carried further along its evolutionary paths, culminates in rites of passage of "global initiation." Externally, this initiation means increasing social differentiation and integration of free and diverse members, functions, and communities. Three-folding, correctly understood, is the visible social actualization of deeply incisive steps in the process of the initiation of humanity since the fifteenth century. It also means greater and more energetic will, and a need for participation and the assuming of more social responsibility, not less. It is central-ization that leaves most people as passive onlookers, uninter-ested, isolated, and estranged, because they feel uninvolved, uninvited, and unwelcome. With the dawning of the age of imperialism, capitalism, and the scientific/industrial revolutions, new economic forces rose to self-consciousness. At the same time, in the American and French revolutions, a democratic state became the place in which human rights consciousness could awaken. Now a third social force begins to become conscious of itself, beyond the market and the state: a force of concern and responsibility for human society as a whole. We see an increasing flow of consciousness and activism into the global social debate that expresses a more mature concern, care, and sense of responsibility for the living earth, human rights, and holistic values and culture.

But hasn't the death of the human, of meaning, of all gods, already been declared, from right, left, and middle? In the last two centuries, this was certainly true. And yet one of the most intriguing symptoms of the recent social activism of civil society is precisely the unexpected and deepening synergy taking place across and between the two major poles of the great social divide, which until now had split progressive humanity into two camps, between which no meeting could take place. We mean here especially the growing together of the "consciousness streams" that focus on cultural values, meanings, and expansion of our cognition, knowledge, and consciousness—that work with the sciences, arts, and religion, with the down-to-earth social activist streams that shoulder the care for earthly humanity and its miseries. The rapprochement of labor and environmental movements observed in Seattle in 1999 and elsewhere is but one symptom of a far wider and still largely unnoticed social and cultural synergy whose significance has yet to be studied.

Economist David Korten describes this process of synergetic convergence as the "globalization of civil society,"[1] based on the growing human awareness that Earth is a living organism, and there exists an "underlying interdependence of the living world." He observes that the global economy, politics, and culture must begin to reflect this fact in social praxis. This sentiment is widely shared the world over. It is a moral intuition as well as a solid scientific fact. As science discovers this truth, millions of free human beings *experience* this fact as a primal motivation in their lives. They are not forced to do so, nor is it written in any bible or other collective rule of conduct. This experience is an individual one. One *can* make this truth into a motivating inspiration for a new social responsibility, even while so many millions in the same society do not. Science may become in this way culturally creative and a source of social motivation, or it may become a source of inspiration for further violent manipulations of life and consciousness. The fact that fast-developing, non-materialistic natural and human sciences are available today to support cultural and social evolution is indeed of the greatest significance for the future of global civil society. However, there is and will be nothing obligatory or deterministic about it. Quite to the contrary, continuous enhancements of ever more powerful materialistic innovations will demand the enhancement of our faculties of intellectual and moral judgment.

Undoubtedly materialism is here to stay, as it is part and parcel of the deeper spiritual origins of the present stage of human evolution. It will remain a necessary practical, social, and cultural motivating force, expressing itself in refined or coarse ways, using fantastic and ingenious scientific and technological creativity. And while its motivation is secured for the long evolutionary term, and while it will not diminish its hold on human civilization, one thing is clear: New and unforeseeable spiritual and cultural sources for social and cultural transformation are and will be strongly present alongside it. The fundamental change occurring now is not the miraculous disappearance of materialistic civilization in the clouds of a rosy New Age paradise, as some dreamers would have it, but increasingly more *balanced* struggles with its ever-growing influences.

Hence, social activism must not remain the realm of opinion, ideology, or subjective moral sentiment, justified as these are in many cases. When one of the most common concepts in natural scientific discourse today is "self-organization" of physical, chemical systems and living organisms, perhaps the time is not far away in which scientists will realize that the human is not less self-organized. And will social scientists and politicians not understand, finally, that in the third cultural, social sector, every school, hospital, and farm must become also self-organizing? Today, because the sciences have been so deeply transformed, social activism can be thoroughly permeated with scientifically based and expanded consciousness, as it could not be in the days of Marx or sociologist Max Weber. When natural science can teach us about self-organization, creative emergence, dynamic universal formative forces, and holistic mind-body-environment integration and synergy, what are the human and social sciences going to teach us next?

After two centuries of being told that the terms "science" and "consciousness" or "spirit" were impossible to combine, we may assert that they are not. In 1987, neurologists Walter Freeman and Christine Skarda changed our conception of our thought processes, and taught us some new, basic lessons about the individual and social-human condition, namely "how brains make chaos in order to make sense of the world."[2] Shaping concepts and representations concerning reality is a creative, emergent process, and "truth" is our free creation, as we are actively engaged in real life when we research, experiment, and know. We are, in our whole nature, part of the world, and the more we learn that the ways in which our minds and hearts are "embodied" in the physical, biological, and social and cosmic environments, the more we learn that, conversely, "mind is everywhere." Intelligence is not a possession of spatial-temporal Cartesian hermits, locked up inside the ultimate, non-permeable borders of their skins. Instead, it but lives, weaves, and becomes in and through us everywhere. This revolutionary scientific conception, stated forcefully by Gregory Bateson[3] and creatively and experimentally demonstrated by Maturana and Varela and the Santiago[4] school, is changing social life and social organization, and will enhance the process of individuation, decentralization, differentiation, and conscious social integration. Current models and concepts of selfhood, brain, mind, and consciousness depict a "self" that is internally open to the infinite creativity of chaos, because it is evolutionarily integrated with the emergent properties of a vastly complex and forever wild and surprising universal whole.

The social significance of this change will not escape us if we remember that until recently the epistemological justification for capitalism and socialism, liberalism and communism, nationalism and fascism alike was positivist scientism. The most reactionary regimes, and the most neo-liberal, new-imperial social philosophies, took pains to ground their ideologies in the scientific materialism of the nineteenth century, be it Marxist, Darwinist, or Freudian, and its various intellectual and social hybrids. For example, it is not hard to prove that, our judgment concerning the historical merits and role of socialism notwithstanding, the most ambitious impulse for social transformation in modern times was based on a Marxist—not to say Leninist-Stalinist and Maoist—social-historical version of nineteenth-century natural science that sought to prove that materialism is the primary fact and moving power in human history. (Liberal, neo-liberal, and "humanistic" beliefs in progress were no less materialistic, of course, but were rarely as honest in proclaiming their commitment to the same materialistic metaphysics of the late nineteenth century.)

The rather dramatic historical change occurring right now, which has been taking place since the 1960s but has reached a greater maturity today, is *the growing realization on the part of progressive humanistic social movements and activists that no true social transformation can be supported by a physicalist and reductionist metaphysics.* Many of them have experienced most strongly what others have known for some time, namely that "spirit matters"—that, cosmically speaking, consciousness, awareness, intelligence, creativity, and emergence are the qualities and forces that make the "real" stuff of suns, galaxies, and planet Earth. "The driving force of evolution," writes Fritjof Capra, "according to the emerging new theory, is to be found not in the chance events of random mutations, but in life's inherent tendency to create novelty, in the spontaneous emergence of increasing complexity and order."[5] What the right, left, and liberal-democratic middle never had before our time is, as Stuart Kauffman says, "[t]his theory of life's origins . . . rooted in an unrepentant holism, born not of mysticism, but of mathematical necessity. Life emerged whole, not piecemeal, and has remained so."[6]

The great yet silent revolution of the end of the last century is that the practice of far deeper self-transformation is already beginning to have a marked influence on many cultural and social domains of life. As Peter Senge suggested, the new dynamic systems' view of physics and biology changes entirely the ways in which our business and corporate organizational formative-social processes are understood.[7] We have today a qualitatively vast number of seriously committed and creative individuals working in the cultural spheres of the sciences, arts, religion, education, medicine, innovative business, and technology, and many of them are increasingly engaged in effecting deep structural social change in economics and politics as well. While our corporate, political, and media establishments the world over continue to caricature and degrade the true spirit of our times, far-reaching creative social transformation is occurring on the social periphery, and in due course it will transform the center and usher in a new social order.

The synergy or convergence between the "spiritualists" and "realists," between matter and spirit, individual and society, and inner and outer modes of experiencing and creating the world, is indeed happening. The coming together in increased resonance of manifold communities and subcultures based on expanded science, philosophy, art, and consciousness on the one hand, and those based on social, political, and economic activism on the other, is perhaps the most important phenomenon in the recent and emergent process of global civil society. And the more this process intensifies, the stronger will be the cultural-spiritual power of civil society to engage the economic and political sectors in creative social tri-sectoral relationships.

What, therefore, is the spiritual origin of the present social transformation, the emergence of global civil society as part of a threefold global social order? A truth that may still sound like a fantastic delusion in the ears of the old ideologically committed activism is that unless a person has experienced the first basic lessons of daily, individual, and freely practiced *self-transformation* (becoming), he or she can contribute very little to a positive transformation of society. And, logically and practically, how could we have believed for so long that it could be otherwise? Can a reformed society be more reformed than each and all of its members? As a matter of fact, as both history and social psychology have amply demonstrated, societies tend to gravitate toward the lowest and not the highest common denominator. Only a conscious individual practice of self-transformation, exercised by each person according to his or her free initiative, can counter this collective drive to lower levels. Social plans and programs are easily produced, but embodying them in personal and mutual transformation is far more difficult. A social community has a chance of moving truly forward only if each member is a strong agent of self-transformation, and therefore of social transformation.

Didn't psychologist Carl Jung already suggest the reason for the horrors that must inevitably result from so many "revolutions" carried out by people who never truly revolutionized their inner psyches? After the twentieth century, no social idealism should be seriously considered as truly future-oriented that is not based on *transformed people*. Don't we have sufficient evidence of what comes about when revolutions and revolutionaries look at the mirror—when the hangover mists dissipate in the "morning after the revolution"—and see the monster of annihilation and rage gazing back? As Jung admonished, "Today humanity, as never before, is split into two apparently irreconcilable halves. The psychological rule says that when an inner situation is not made conscious, it happens outside as fate. That is to say, when the individual remains undivided and does not become conscious of his or her inner opposite, the world must perforce act out the conflict and be turned into opposing halves."[8] It is not the failed revolutions but the successful ones, the realized ideologies from left, right, and center, that have created the unimaginable horrors perpetrated by fascism, National Socialism, communism, and elite globalization. This well-trodden way is saturated with the blood spilled by the best intentions.

Jung's psychological rule can offer a hint as to the cause of this historical process: our repressed inner split, our unrecognized and unconscious inner opposite (also known as our "shadow" or "double"), that becomes our social self—that is, our own unredeemed and destructive human nature. We may be able, though this is rather rare, to suppress our demons in our interactions with our immediate surroundings, but then our repressed death and power drives will take that much more dominant a shape in the greater social world, to become institutionalized in our "revolutionary" social and cultural institutions—in so many gulags, concentration camps, or transnational corporations—that devastate the environment and enslave billions of people economically, socially, and culturally. We should have learned by now at least to identify in ourselves the potential for those messianic, apocalyptic, semi-secular utopias of rage, doom, and totalitarianism, under whatever social reformatory vocabulary and costume they are hiding themselves.

Visionary historian William Irwin Thompson pointed this out in his outstanding little book *Evil and World Order*; namely that there is a deeper structural common ground that underlies the otherwise seemingly opposite and socially most devastating utopian ideologies of the twentieth century. They all lacked a non-materialistic science of human consciousness and spiritual human development of the stages of self-transformation that we as individuals can experience if we seriously strive for greater responsibility for our personal and social being and becoming. In denying this expanded scientific view, this cultural power, the activists of the twentieth century found themselves helpless in the face of the relentless historical realization of Jung's psychological principle. What they repressed became social and cultural history in so many ways. And this is so because, as Thompson aptly observes:

> There can be no love in one who does not love himself, and one can only love himself if he has the compassion that grows out of the terrifying confrontation with one's own self. To look into one's shadow is to learn compassion for the shadow of others, and if one has no compassion for himself, then he can have no compassion for others. If you hate yourself with a fierce loathing—as Faulkner would say, "in the fury of abhorrence"—you may try to turn from your own shadow in a campaign to do good, not for love, but to rescue your ego and convince yourself that you are not evil. In the eyes of how many world-transforming activists do we not see dissonance, anxiety, fear and self-loathing? They would reform the world, but they cannot even reform themselves, much less quit smoking. They are running from evil, the evil they have not confronted in terror inside themselves, and thus their unbalanced idealism is inflicting the Terror upon all of us.[9]

Now, neo-liberal globalization and postmodern imperialism are as utopian and totalitarian as communism. The most powerful materialistic utopia didn't collapse with communism, as is commonly believed. On the contrary, it marches on as never before, lacking rudimentary spiritual self-knowledge, and therefore continuing to inflict the social devastation described above in the name of scientific, economic, and social "progress." Such liberal progressive humanism that doesn't pass through the "needle's eye" test of somber self-knowledge is bound to repeat the twentieth century's catastrophes on a much greater global scale in the twenty-first century. And the backlash as we experienced on September 11, 2001 is but the shape of things to come.

A noteworthy feature of Alston Chase's instructive study, "Harvard and the Making of the Unabomber," is that Chase doesn't limit himself to the single case of the Unabomber and the horrendous mind control experiments on students in Harvard's psychology department. He sheds penetrating light on the otherwise well-hidden intellectual and spiritual roots of the originally western intellectual "culture of despair." "From the humanists," he writes, "we learned that science threatens civilization. From the scientists we learned that science cannot be stopped. Taken together, they implied that there was no hope. General Education had created at Harvard a culture of despair." He quotes a saying of Bertrand Russell's that characterizes a central nerve of this highly advanced and sophisticated, liberal, and technologically brilliant culture: "Only on the firm foundation of unyielding despair, can the soul's habitation henceforth be safely built."[10]

Russell, like so many of the intellectual, liberal, scientifically trained minds of the first half of the last century, believes that the human soul in the modern age can find its safe home in the universe only if it does not yield to the despair that the modern conception of life and existence inspires. But in what way can such a conception be justified? Looking backward at the last century we may try now to understand the cultural and social mood that inspired such existential feelings and judgments. It is said that we are to be motivated by a culture of despair, not yielding to this despair but fighting on to overcome and conquer in an external, material way every aspect of human life and destiny. "In a dark and infinitely non-human universe, the evolution of Earth, with its life, consciousness, culture, is an unlikely, random event, without any meaning"— so goes the main narrative of the liberal, socialist, capitalist, communist, and fascist "humanistic" culture of despair, and so it has gone since the end of the nineteenth century. What humans create on the earth, their ideas and ideals, their moral values, the arts, sciences, and technology, is all dust-born and advances inexorably towards its unavoidable death through universal entropy. Life is wholly meaningless and despairing, but we will continue nevertheless, building our culture of despair on unyielding despair."

But can we find a way to understand the deeper meaning behind this phase of individuation? Is there any meaning to this seeming quintessence of all meaninglessness? Not much is accomplished in mere logical or philosophical "refutation" of physicalism and reductionist scientism. We must be able to *understand* it and not merely refute it. *Why* does despair become a culture, and culture become despair, at this stage of the evolution of human consciousness? Existential despair can yield itself to such an interpretation if viewed in context as a stage in the evolutionary process of the individuation of consciousness. In this way it doesn't show only its negative aspect as the outer limit of our progressive powers beyond which nobody will ever dare to venture; it reveals inherent and powerful initiatory energy, a dynamism that can destroy, but create new worlds of hope as well.

How can we integrate this stage of evolution, which crystallized and hardened historically into a permanent cultural mood in the western culture of despair, in the greater flow of the individuation process? We can do so, provided we are ready to consider the possibility that the *world conceptions* produced by scientific physicalism, completely apart from the many technological blessings that physicalism bestowed on humanity, may not be capable of providing the ultimate and final truth about the nature of existence. And, what is more, that they reflect a crucial, but rather short, moment in the evolution of human consciousness.

Rudolf Steiner suggested that, at a specific point in human evolution, human consciousness naturally develops cognitive faculties that separate and cut it from the living universe, *because only in this way can the human being become an independent human "I."* Such an evolutionary reasoning was developed also by Owen Barfield,[11] who called the ancient, dreamlike, and pre-scientific state of spiritual consciousness prevalent in older civilizations a consciousness of and objective "original participation," by means of which humans were naturally immersed in the living processes of an intelligent, creative, and meaningful universe. Human beings, Barfield said, separate themselves from this universe very much as a child separates himself or herself from the dreamy world of childhood into the often cold and estranged world of adulthood. But later, as the child matures, he or she rediscovers essential meanings of life on a much higher, free, creative level, because this knowledge is now achieved through individual effort and toil.

It is within the "fold of the self," as cultural historian and philosopher Michel Foucault discovered in his studies of the emergence of subjectivation—"in the interior of the exterior and inversely"—and in phenomenologist Maurice Merleau-Ponty's "the turning back on itself of the visible," that the universe enfolds itself, "involves," in order to make a subject of itself and come to self-consciousness of its infinity. "As a force among forces," wrote Foucault, "man does not fold the forces that compose him without the outside folding itself, and creating a Self within man. . . . [T]he fold of the outside constitutes as Self, while the outside itself forms a coextensive inside. . . . The Self, as self-Being, is determined by the process of subjectification."[12] This is the apex of current global initiation and the real spiritual origin of the force that alone can set limits to elite globalization and its vision of predatory individuation. Here are found the origins of threefold social differentiation and integration. The subjective, isolated Cartesian hermit is indeed a historical cocoon, out of which global initiation emerges. The moderns have prepared this isolation in order to hatch out of it a marvelous human wonder. Here an *interior* societal and cosmic place is prepared, in which profound riddles of cosmic becomings shall become human:

> O, what a world of unseen visions and heard silences, this insubstantial country of the mind! What ineffable essences, these touchless rememberings and unshowable reveries! And the privacy of it all! A secret theater of speechless monologue and prevenient counsel, an invisible mansion of all moods, musings, and mysteries, an infinite resort of disappointments and discoveries. A whole kingdom where each of us reigns reclusively alone, questioning what we will, commanding what we can. A hidden hermitage where we may study out the troubled book of what we have done and yet may do. An introcosm that is more myself than anything I can find in a mirror. This consciousness that is myself of

selves, that is everything, and yet is nothing at all—
what is it? And where did it come from? And why?[13]

Being submerged from the beginning within *given* and
hence coercive meaning, be it God, nature, culture, or any
other collectively given meaning that predates the intellectual
and moral autonomy of the single individual, keeps the human
in a childhood state—blessed, perhaps, but also dependent and
uncreative. Materialism, agnosticism, and atheism are but the
most powerful and ingenious devices created by the evolving
human mind to realize an ever-growing freedom from external
and internal, given and hence coercive meanings—not,
however, in order to declare universal meaninglessness as the
final ontological truth, *but in order to regain meaning freely
and creatively from the emergent cosmos that we are
becoming.* Gilles Deleuze's great achievement is an exact philosophical conceptualization and affirmation of James Joyce's
poetic "Chaosmos"[14] as such a firstborn, integrative sense of
cosmic Selfhood. This Self, however, is global; it views the
living Earth from the most intimate vantage point of the dead
Moon, and marks the extensive inwardness of the human at
the same time as it marks the intensive outside of the cosmos.

This Self does not know a division between a subjective
"inner" world and an objective external world. It is the
reversal of these opposites, inside out and outside in—an infinitely manifold and expanded cosmos "within," and cosmos as
oneself "outside." Postmodern selfhood fulfills modern initiation when this reversal is realized in the sciences, humanities,
arts, philosophy, and a new social order. We are now initiated
into the mysteries of the vast and multifarious circumference
revealed as our inner personal world, and find "the one" inten-
sively experienced in the cosmic circumference.

What the new natural science teaches us is that we harbor within us the creative potentials of our universe, and that the infinite variety and richness that Earth and cosmos spread in space before our eyes is our becoming intelligence writ large. As the belief in universal entropy and the unavoidable warmth death of the human and the cosmos-dominated thermodynamics and the whole of natural science and the humanities in the late nineteenth century wanes, the end of the twentieth century and the beginning of the twenty-first are teeming with vital dynamism, emergent creativity, and a resurrection of wonder and sense of the sacred.

The ability of the modern human mind, beginning in the nineteenth century, to portray the universe, nature, and human nature as wholly devoid of creative intelligence and cosmic spiritual-moral purpose—hence meaningless, random, and despairing—is a positive, most courageous evolutionary step. It leads us today toward a free integration of a much greater spiritual human creativity in a universe, nature, and human nature whose meaningful existence will be rediscovered in far greater radiance than was possible to ancient, atavistic, clairvoyant cognition.

This rediscovery, involving multifaceted, differentiated, and hence freer human individuality, society, and culture, will give expression to independent human co-creativity in the ongoing creative evolution of the universe. The human, passing through the needle eye of individuation, will have discovered within itself the inner creative source of the external universe, and then, as T. S. Eliot noted, "the end of all our exploring," after circling one octave higher in the evolutionary spiral, will be "to arrive where we started" and, through individual freedom, "know the place for the first time."[15] Like scientist and priest Pierre Teilhard de Chardin, Eliot was simply imagining Darwin's theory of evolution through to its natural-spiritual (human) involution. Taking this concept with a grain of post-Darwinian evolutionary thought, the late paleontologist Stephen Jay Gould[16] showed that the human is indeed a perpetual creature of beginnings, because of its evolutionary loyalty to its universal origins. It is therefore not at all a "more developed" animal, but rather a far less developed animal; the human is strongly in-volved. It owes its evolution to a powerful involution that safeguarded it as a juvenile, embryonic, "neotonic ape," growing up and yet preserving its childlike body, mind, and psychological freshness and openness. The human is essentially childlike, universal, and unspecialized. It *preserved* its original humanity, while animals "specialized" and *lost* it in the course of the adaptive struggle for existence.

As economist Hazel Henderson[17] once commented, in evolution successful adaptation means unavoidable downfall and extinction. Only the "unfit," namely, the human, survives and inherits the earth. It masters its environment because it is not mastered by it. The human became human because it resisted animalization—because it renounced strict and rigid specialization and non-reversible physical adaptation: preservation of its agile, pliable, and flexible long childhood, a postponement of maturity, and a lifelong ability to learn and mentally evolve. This is what is called in sacred traditions the "divine spark," the universal image of God that makes up the deeper spiritual nature of the human. In the course of biological evolution, the human successfully specialized in un-specialization. Will it continue to further involve its evolution in this direction in future times?

The lasting value of the natural scientific civilization is not to be found in its materialistic philosophies and worldviews, intellectually sophisticated and logical as they may be, which

are but temporary expressions of one unique and short historical time, but in the abiding achievements of individuation.
While the intellectual-conceptual *contents* of materialistic
worldviews gradually lose their hold on human culture, the
strengthening of self-consciousness, individual free thinking
and conduct, and their past, present, and future social and
cultural fruits, will continue to increase, but will be integrated
into more human and spiritual worldviews. Philosopher Ernst
Cassirer pointed out that legend, myth, religious revelations,
and folklore are truthful descriptions of reality no less than the
later scientific ones.[18] They should not be arrogantly conceived
to be ignorant "projections" and "animations" on the screen
of an otherwise meaningless universe, created out of the
wishful fantasies of primitives who had not yet discovered the
ultimate ground of meaninglessness and despair that the light
of modern science and technology reveal, but rather as
primeval modes of cognition intimately woven into the very
fabric of universal and human life. This conception of the
evolution of human consciousness does not naively take the
recent subjective changes in human cognition to mean that,
because we no longer imaginatively perceive angels and gods,
elemental spirits and human souls as spiritual realities, they
"never existed" and are mere products of uneducated fantasy.
Rather, it is open to the more logical possibility that for a short
historical span of evolution humans lost the atavistic soul
faculties that enabled them to perceive the world spiritually,
because if such atavism had persisted, the human self never
would have been able to awaken to itself as an independent self
and creator of a social order that would reflect this freedom
and creative possibility. This approach explains convincingly
that in order to develop a clear-cut sense of individual self-

hood, rationality, and individual moral judgment, the older powers of cognition had to pass away.

However, once grounded in an individualized and estranged human psyche, society, and culture, these powers are not eliminated but transformed, resulting in a synergy between modern science, rationality, democracy, and renewed spiritual cognition that will not simply regain and repeat wisdom treasures of older spiritual traditions, but will expand capabilities to entirely new horizons through the new ability to penetrate material civilization with spiritual consciousness. We will gain the ability to build a society and culture that can integrate the material and the spiritual aspects of our Being in a certain unstable and emergent harmony.

We should, at the very least, entertain the possibility that this evolutionary narrative makes sense, and that, if correct, it is the only one that can positively explain the evolutionary need for materialism and reductionism, and thereby shed hopeful and positive light on the culture of despair. We may then discover that the universe, Earth, nature, and human nature are not random, meaningless, or even absurd "in themselves," but that *we* in this specific historical moment experience them as such.

We are all already despair's children, sons and daughters of twentieth-century holocausts and horrors. For us, the culture of despair is the ground from which, phoenix-like, our initiation springs forth. Paradoxically, an unyielding despair cannot provide a firm foundation for the human soul, but "yielding despair" can, because it is despair as a creative precondition for the inner, free, and fully self-conscious rediscovery of ancient as well as wholly new meanings of existence. Authentic future spirituality that seeks to become a powerful source for social transformation must indeed steel its cognitive and moral

forces in the core of the culture of despair. The grave of European civilization, opened in the course of twentieth century, is
our permanent future heritage and remains our cultural
wound, a perpetual admonition goading us to self-knowledge
and transformation, deeply branded into our twenty-first-
century souls. Are we to embody our wound freely, as an act
of redemption and healing, or run away from it in self-hatred,
blame, repression, or utopian elite globalization?

If we freely choose to venture into the labyrinth of the
culture of despair, and become fully versed in philosophers
Martin Heidegger's and Jean-Paul Sartre's existential *Gewor-
fenheit* (Throwness), we do so because it offers us a succinct
summary of the nineteenth- and twentieth-century existential
experience. It offers wholly unique experiences and faculties to
the human soul. This experience—a modern, but now historical, external-social version of the ancient descending into the
underworld, of death and resurrection—is in line with the
descent into the sub-human realities of human nature in the
sense of Jung's, Steiner's, and Thompson's admonition to true
self-knowledge. It can provide the groundless ground, the
abyss, based on which we can practice the *"Sprung in den Ur-
Sprung"* (leap into the original source) that the later Heidegger
contemplated, trying to recover from his own and his culture's
moral and intellectual fall. As the mystics who were initiated
into the Eleusian Greek mysteries of the earth mother Demeter
had, in the course of their living Initiation, to descend into
their own personal hell, discover again their own fallen soul
(Persephone), transform their own sub-earthly and "evil" soul
force (Pluto-Hades), and come back to physical life transformed through the god of resurrection (Dionysus), so must
humanity as a whole undergo its initiatory individuation at the
present stage of the evolution of human consciousness. Out of

the grave of civilization of the twentieth century, twenty-first-century humanity may experience a true resurrection.

This process is not mere Hegelian logical dialectics and cannot be intellectually known and secured *in advance;* it must be *experienced* again and again each day in the struggle to understand the meaning of what seem to be the insurmountable limits of our present consciousness. It means a courageous plunging into the labyrinth to confront face to face the power in us that creates meaninglessness, the intellect that must constantly "murder to dissect"[19] (Wordsworth) in order to set us free from an abundantly meaningful universe. After steeling free individuality in the loneliness of the culture of despair, we must resurrect the human soul to new universally meaningful existence in the immeasurable creativity, wisdom, and benevolence of a spiritual and intelligent universe. Death appears as the portal of modern initiation itself, crowning individuation with its ultimate sense—"die and become" (Goethe). "It is at this mobile and precise point, where all events gather together in one that transmutation happens," maintains Deleuze, "where dying is the negation of death. . . . [T]he impersonality of dying no longer indicates only the moment when I disappear outside myself, but rather the moment when death loses itself in itself, and also the figure which the most singular life takes on in order to substitute itself for me."[20]

If initiation is to be taken seriously, and not only as philosophical concept, we must understand that it means humanity is advancing towards a future in which, once again, the gods will be with us. Once they had to withdraw, to eclipse their dazzling light and omnipotent power, in order to let our egos mature and shine forth. However, now they appear as transcendent, immanent presences, in and through our own selves, illuminating our freedom and enhancing our individual, free moral existence. When we become strong, intelligent, and all-powerful, they speak to us as companions, gently reminding us of our divine heritage, essence, and goals.

So the angels are back with us—and in America they appear in an American manner, that is, with refreshing directness, humanness, and humor. For example, Dr. Michael Abrams has learned to communicate with them in the emergency room as he attends to dying patients, and has discussed the riddles of existence with them. What is most remarkable is the freshness and vitality of the angels' discourse, their uncompromising holistic logic, and divine sense of humor. If we wish to think through to the other side of despair and meaninglessness—to individuation, death, and resurrection of consciousness—then such a dialogue between an American emergency room physician and his guiding angels should be taken into consideration:

The Angels [commenting on a previous question]:
You assume that you and God are two different beings and have two different agendas. This is simply not the case!

Abrams
Are you saying that I am in fact God?

The Angels
(Great laughter.) *Of course!*

Abrams
Why is that funny?

The Angels
It's funny to hear God asking, in that kind of suspicious, accusatory tone, if he is in fact God. Only you would set up such a fascinating joke on yourself.
Silence

[. . . .]

The Angels
You still don't understand. We are you, the real you. If we get involved—and you should make no mistake about it, we do get involved in your lives—we do so as extensions of your own will. But that's just it, way down deep, your will and God's will are one and the same. While you are down there in that guise playing that role, you are not aware of this, but it is nonetheless true.

When you think a thought or pray a prayer . . . that thought goes out into the universe and begins to take form. You, Spirit, and all of Spirit's messengers and agents, all of us are connected together in one milieu, one gigantic coordinated field of consciousness.

This field of consciousness is like a fertile garden. Thoughts planted in its soil germinate and grow into real concrete circumstances. All of us—humans, angels, and Infinite intelligence—are the seeds, the garden, and the gardener, simultaneously.

(Laughter.) It's very hard to explain to a human but that's how it is set up. That is how Spirit has constructed itself so that it can constantly generate

*new and different realities, realities that keep
growing and evolving.*

(Pause.) *Another way of looking at it is that
angels don't answer your prayers, we are your
prayers. We are living, fluid forms of light that
emanate from mind. We respond to God's mind and
to yours. Again, they are one and the same.*[21]

Russell's abyss of despair is an important existential
achievement for consciousness that evolves toward a greater
sense of individual freedom and responsibility. In the past such
states of extreme desperation, meaninglessness, and loneliness
were consciously enacted as the most demanding tests of the
human soul and spirit powers in all serious ancient, spiritual
rites of passage and initiation. That humanity as a whole
underwent in the course of the nineteenth and twentieth
centuries a descent into its own self-created and self-imposed
hell is an historical fact; that it can in the twenty-first century
learn how to transform this descent into an existential initiation and a blessing for its present evolution can become a fully
justified and fruitful foundation for a fundamentally more
human culture and society.

*Decentralized, threefold society is an expression of decen-
tralized, manifold, and autonomous selfhood.* As more and
more people over the Earth experience the above-described
stage of individuation, they will strive to create the social
formations that will best express their maturing individual
freedom. As the democratic modern nation state externally
embodied an inner dramatic transformation of consciousness,
allowing greater masses of people to express their advancing
individuation through a democratic social process, so today,
not only in the political sector but also in economic and

cultural matters, the individual is freeing itself. As each free individual seeks to be directly involved in his or her economic, political, and cultural community, threefoldness will come about as naturally as centralized democracy emerged out of older authoritarian social structures. Threefold social differentiation and integration is the social environment in which the next stage in the evolution of human consciousness is going to manifest itself.

Notes

1. See David Korten, *When Corporations Rule the World* (Bloomfield, CT: Kumarian Press, Inc., 2001).
2. Christine A. Skarda and Walter J. Freeman, "How brains make chaos in order to make sense of the world," *Behavioral and Brain Sciences* (1987)10, pp. 161–195. "We propose that the brain relies on chaotic as opposed to steady or random activity for several purposes: Chaos constitutes the basic form of collective neural activity for all perceptual processes and functions as a controlled source of noise, as a means to ensure continual access to previously learned sensory patterns, and as the means for learning new sensory patterns."
3. See Gregory and Mary Catherine Bateson, *Steps to an Ecology of Mind: Collected Essays in Anthropology, Psychiatry, Evolution, and Epistemology* (Chicago: University of Chicago Press, 2000), p. 436: "The individual mind is immanent but not only in the body. It is immanent also in the pathways and messages outside the body; and there is a larger Mind of which the individual mind is only a sub-system. This larger Mind is comparable to God and is perhaps what some people mean by 'God,' but it is still immanent in the total interconnected social system and planetary ecology."
4. Humberto R. Maturana and Francisco J. Varela, *Autopoiesis and Cognition: The Realization of the Living* (Boston Studies in the Philosophy of Science, V. 42), Dordrecht, Holland: D Reidel Pub Co; 1991.
5. Fritjof Capra, *The Web of Life* (New York: Doubleday, 1997), pp. 227–8.
6. Stuart A. Kauffman, *At Home in the Universe* (New York: Oxford University Press, 1996), p. 69.
7. Peter M. Senge, *The Fifth Discipline: The Art and Practice of the Learning Organization* (New York: Currency/Doubleday, 1994).
8. C. G. Jung, *Collected Works*, 9, 11 para 126 (New York: Routledge and Kegan Paul, Ltd., 1959).
9. William Irwin Thompson, *Evil and World Order* (New York: Harper & Row, 1976), pp. 86–7.

10. Alston Chase, "Harvard and the Making of the Unabomber," in *The Atlantic Monthly*, June 2000. The quotation by Bertrand Russell comes from "A Free Man's Worship," which is in Volume 12, Collected Papers of Bertrand Russell, entitled *Contemplation and Action*, 1902–1914 (New York: Routledge, 1985).
11. See Owen Barfield, *Saving the Appearances: A Study in Idolatry* (Middletown, CT: Wesleyan University Press, 1988).
12. Quoted in Gilles Deleuze, *Foucault* (Minneapolis, MN: University of Minnesota Press, 1988), p. 114.
13. Julian Jaynes, *The Origins of Consciousness in the Breakdown of the Bicameral Mind* (Boston: Houghton Mifflin, 2000).
14. See Umberto Eco, *The Aesthetics of Chaosmos: The Middle Ages of James Joyce* (Cambridge, MA: Harvard University Press, 1989).
15. T. S. Eliot, "Little Gidding," *Four Quartets*, 1943.
16. See Stephen Jay Gould, *The Structure of Evolutionary Theory* (Cambirdge, MA: Harvard University Press, 2002).
17. See Hazel Henderson, *Beyond Globalization: Shaping a Sustainable Global Economy* (Bloomfield, CT: Kumarian Press, Inc., 1999).
18. See Ernst Cassirer, *Language and Myth* (New York & London: Harper & Bros., 1946).
19. William Wordsworth, "Tables Turned."
20. Gilles Deleuze, *Logic of Sense* (New York: Columbia University Press, 1990), p. 153.
21. Michael Abrams, *The Evolution Angel: An Emergency Physician's Lessons with Death and the Divine* (Boulder, CO: Abundance Media, 2000), pp. 66–67.

Chapter 16

❧

Synergy Between Social Activism and Spiritualized Science and Consciousness

THE INCREASED EMANCIPATION AND INDIVIDUATION OF humanity is reflected in its changing social and cultural forms. New social forms express a deep structural transformation of the collective human soul and spirit. As medieval universal monarchy was replaced by the modern nation state, so today we witness an equivalent social transformation in the emerging tri-sectoral social structure. Individuation carried further must lead to increased social and cultural freedom and free association and integration in economic, political, and cultural-spiritual life. Threefold society is growing out of the same roots from which the modern democratic state grew, and signifies the same evolutionary thrust toward human individuation, responsibility, and free social conditions. Hence we may expect that the more individuation matures, the more explicit will be the relations between spiritual transformations of the deep collective structures and their reflection in appropriate external social formations.

Looked at on a deeper psychological and spiritual level, individuation is a "triple-edged sword" that represents a decisive evolutionary decision that must increasingly be confronted by each individual and society as a whole. Once released from the supporting sustenance of collective systems, the individual can take one of the following paths.

- One can "harden" oneself and isolate oneself from the universe and other human beings. This can be done through extreme forms of materialism as well as escapist spiritualism or through a unique amalgamation of both.

- One can revert backward—or even forward—to older or new forms of mass or group consciousness at the price of giving up personal responsibility and freedom. This can be done both through a "return" to old collective and hierarchical social-cultural-religious structures, fundamentalism, and anti-modernism, or through immersing oneself in the mass materialism of western consumerist culture, surrendering to the hegemonic global rule of the "bolshevism of capital."

- One can use one's freedom for self-transformation guided by mature individual consciousness. This can be done by developing a balanced individual and social "breathing" rhythm that regulates inward and outward movements. Inward "in-breathing" into self-knowledge and self-transformation, and external "out-breathing" into social activism and practice become mutually inclusive and enhancing. The more integrated the two movements become, the more mature will become this new social-cultural "yoga" practice, which will increasingly combine the social with the cultural-spiritual, building the strong and flexible conscious backbone for global civil society.

With this perspective in mind, paradoxical as it may still appear in the light of older reductionist social and cultural conceptions, it shouldn't surprise us to realize that a more consciously explicit synergy is taking place today between the spiritually oriented cultural streams—new trends and movements in science, art, medicine, education, and so forth on the one hand, and political and economic strategies and policies on the other—that is in accord with the most essential thrust of the evolution of human consciousness in our time. Both human rights consciousness and the advocacy for human-centered economy are experiencing today a fresh infusion of forces from the deeper sources of human consciousness, minds, and hearts. Culture and social activism are emanating from the selfsame sources of moral-spiritual innovation and motivation that work within free human souls and spirits. If we take this possibility seriously—a possibility that is a cause of greatest concern for all the elites of our times—we may realize that the emergence of global civil society is a wholly justified evolutionary social change that is here to stay. This means also that the possibility for true social transformation lies in a creative moral-social revitalization of the first two social sectors by means of the new and younger forces of a *third sector*: the emerging global social sector of free civil initiative and action based on a radical spiritualization of the most basic philosophical and scientific paradigms and narratives.

Only by means of free, independent moral-social initiative and responsibility that strives to transform the social meaning of business and finance and to reawaken human-rights awareness can a new relation be established between the equally justified needs of capitalism and socialism. After all, capitalism and socialism represent two historically determined ways to confront the same changes brought about in global economy by means of scientific and technological advancements. The sector of law and human rights, on which the democratic state is founded, and the economic sector, which administers production, consumption, and exchange of goods, can be gradually regained by the *whole* human individuality and by the interests of society *as a whole*, only if mediated and permeated by a third sector that is becoming increasingly conscious of its unique identity. The foundation of this third sector is not a social "class" (the workers), as Marxists believed beginning at the end of the nineteenth century. It is not a bourgeois concept of civil society as middle-class, guarding the selfish social interests of the economically privileged (that is, civil society as "the backbone of capitalist liberal society"). As long as we approach modern civil society with these obsolete social theoretical concepts, we will miss its central uniqueness, which lies exactly in the fact that for a first historical moment, humans are beginning to experience society as a whole human affair. Of what value and use are those scholastic sociological categories, if Abraham Maslow's "self actualizing people" and Paul Ray's "cultural creatives" practice Capra's social ecology and Korten's "living economies for a living planet," and are increasingly populating the ranks of social activists?[1] It appears that social activists show a growing understanding of the nature, origins, and creative power of emergent, complex, and dynamic, natural social, and spiritual levels of existence, disclosed in the new sciences, becoming more appreciative of the creative power of consciousness in the formation of values, meanings, and cultures. At the other social pole, scientific, cultural, religious, and consciousness-centered movements and people are beginning to understand the need for alternative economic, financial, industrial, and commercial social formations.

The bridging of the abyss between the social and spiritual, in both directions at once, tremendously increases the power of civil society as a culturally creative influence in global social life. If we are right in our analysis, this may mean that a certain threshold in societal evolution may have been irrevocably crossed. There can no longer be any serious doubt that the strength of human freedom and moral responsibility developed markedly in the last decades of the twentieth century. The emergence of global civil society shows clearly that many millions of people all over the world are awakening to their ability to exercise social responsibility and power. As Michael Hardt and Antonio Negri have pointed out:

> [Traditional] civil society is absorbed in the state, but the consequence of this is an explosion of the elements that were previously coordinated and mediated in civil society. Resistances are no longer marginal but active in the center of a society that opens up in networks; the individual points are singularized in a thousand plateaus. . . . [This] is therefore the paradox of a power that, while it unifies and envelops within itself every element of social life . . . at that very moment reveals a new context, a new milieu of maximum plurality and uncontainable singularization—a milieu of the event.[2]

The crucial point is that civil society develops synchronously with individuation of the human spirit and its correlative, the decentralization of social life. Individuation does make a difference in social life: it differentiates three autonomous sectors of social responsibility and activity: the economy, polity, and culture. The celebrated "difference" of post-structuralist deconstruction and postmodern philosophy finds here its first social realization. Individual difference builds and spiritualizes the differentiated social sectors. While striving to decentralize the centralized power of the state and to reverse the pyramidal-hierarchical structures of economic power, we must also strive to integrate individual and institutional social activism with "expansion of consciousness," creating emergent, creative pathways of cognition, in which sciences, arts, and all other cultural-spiritual activities are transformed. Without a wholly concrete, practical, and deeply incisive self-transformation of *the social transformers themselves* coupled with corresponding threefold, economic, political, and cultural strategies, civil society is doomed to repeat the fate of its other well-meaning forerunners. A spiritually transformative paradigm shift must penetrate today down to the very foundations of material civilization.

As a result, the creative pressure of civil society on all social levels is felt strongly in the highest echelons of global elite power. Now that they have strongly experienced the irrepressible and irreversible power of global civil society, how are they going to deal with it? What are the ways by means of which they are currently striving to engage, cooperate with, or co-opt civil society?

Notes

1. See Abraham Maslow, *Toward a Psychology of Being* (New York: Van Nostrand Reinhold, 1968); Paul Ray and Sherry Ruth Anderson, *The Cultural Creatives: How 50 Million People Are Changing the World* (New York: Three Rivers Press, 2001); and Korten, see www.pcdf.org/living_economics/ (viewed on October 13, 2003).
2. Michael Hardt and Antonio Negri, *Empire* (Cambridge, MA: Harvard University Press, 2000), p. 25.

Chapter 17

❧

The Battle of Seattle and its Aftermath: Elite Views of Civil Society

THE EMINENTLY DESTRUCTIVE EFFECTS OF ELITE GLOBALIZA-
tion on many essential parameters of human life have caused a
widespread mobilization of intellectual, cultural, and civil
resistance to elite globalization. We described above the emergence of a new, postmodern social power, distinct from traditional liberal civil society. Central spokespeople of leading elite
institutions were quick to recognize this emergence—quicker,
indeed, than many of the sociologists and political scientists
committed to old modernist social paradigms. I believe, therefore, that empirically, at least, this is a fact beyond dispute
today, whatever our judgment concerning it: that civil society
is the third sector of an emerging threefold local, national, and
global postmodern social order, and is a symptomatic phenomenon of the present stage of cultural and societal individuation
and planetary initiation

The powerful impact of a more confident and self-conscious
third sector (civil society) has already made a difference in
central global economic and trade policy in its capacity as
"defender of culture." Before the much more widely publicized
"Battle of Seattle," its effect was felt in connection with the
largely unknown negotiations about the so-called Multilateral

Agreement on Investment (MAI). So powerful, in fact, was the impact of NGOs and, more specifically, of civil society organizations (CSOs), that the financial-political global elite establishment has had to take their activity seriously into account, demonstrating historical and social alertness to emerging trends in the spiritual-cultural life of modern humanity.

The Power Shift
In an article entitled "The Power Shift" in the January/February 1997 volume of *Foreign Affairs,* a senior fellow at the Council on Foreign Relations, Jessica T. Mathews, wrote:

> The end of the cold war has brought . . . a novel redistribution of power among states, market, and civil society. . . . [NGOs] deliver more official development assistance than the entire U.N. system. In many countries they are delivering the services—in urban and rural community development, education, and health care—that faltering governments can no longer manage. . . . [I]ncreasingly, the NGOs are able to push around even the largest governments.

Mathews believes that civil society, via its NGOs, entered irrevocably into the power structure of global society at the Earth Summit in Rio de Janeiro in 1992:

> NGOs set the original goal of negotiating an agreement to control greenhouse gases long before governments were ready to do so, proposed most of its structure and content, and lobbied and mobilized public pressure to force through a pact that virtually no one else thought possible when the talks began....

As a result, things speeded up remarkably. Mathews relates that delegates completed the framework of a global climate accord in a remarkably brief 16 months, over the oppositions of the three energy superpowers: the United States, Russia, and Saudi Arabia. "The Treaty entered into force in record time just two years later . . . with potentially enormous implications for every economy."

An even more remarkably successful campaign of NGOs in the years 1996–98 led to the abolition, at least in their original and draconian form, of the largely secret dealings of the leading world financial institutions and corporations to achieve MAI. This great battle took place far away from commercial and so-called free media, and found only very rare and belated expression. Only by linking to the Internet, where thousands of NGOs were actively cooperating and managing this campaign, could one gain an inkling of the enormity of the efforts and counter-efforts being undertaken. The second major mouthpiece of the global elite establishment, *Foreign Policy* magazine, dedicated a special study to this phenomenon in its fall 1998 volume under the title, "Global Impact—NGOs in the Field."

Foreign Policy magazine, as we have often been told, was founded in order to give expression to the so-called "liberal" wing in the establishment as a counterbalance to the older *Foreign Affairs*. However, as is the case more often than not, on essential strategic political and economic issues, we would be hard pressed to find real differences. "Witness the 'victory' that NGOs recently achieved," wrote its editor, "when they stymied efforts by the Organization for Economic Cooperation and Development, a group made up of the world's 29 major industrial countries, to draft the MAI, a treaty setting common standards for the treatment of foreign investment by host countries." This first major victory of civil society, one that should have been warmly welcomed by anyone honestly striving towards democratization and accountability for the global economic and monetary system, is presented here as something to be sorry about. And the opening of public debate over a document that would have affected all walks of life for billions of otherwise uninformed people around the globe was particularly deplored. The editor continued, "[H]undreds of NGOs of all stripes, sizes, nationalities, and interests rallied against the MAI, using one of the most important drivers of globalization, the Internet, to derail an initiative designed to facilitate another of globalization's most powerful forces, foreign investment."

Understandably, the author doesn't try to make explicit the *reason* for "facilitating" globalization's "most powerful forces, foreign investment" by means of the MAI agreement. If speaking truthfully, he would have had to tell his readers that, to take but one example, the very same financial conditions that led—by "unfortunate coincidence"—to the economic and social disintegration of many southeast Asian countries during the Asian economic meltdown of 1997–98 would have found in the MAI a secure global legal framework. Far from preventing such disasters, the MAI would have institutional-ized their causes legally and internationally, and would have made explicit what was implicit in the current global financial architecture: the old-new social Darwinism put into ever more expanded and efficient practice.

However, the rise of global civil society has caused from the beginning a certain split in the ranks of elite globalizers. Beside those who continue to complain and deride civil society, we find others who try to accommodate themselves to the new conditions. For example, we can read such opinions as this one appearing in the globally syndicated *International Herald Tribune*:

> They [the NGOs] are called the third sector, along-
> side the state and private sector. They offer a new
> channel to introduce both social responsibility and a
> democratic approach where either government or
> commerce has always dominated. . . .[T]hey are an
> energetic force in the conduct of international rela-
> tions and the spread of civil society across borders.

We see here the growing awareness of a third perspective on social questions, one that is gaining ground among those who have for years opposed the very possibility of such development. Others show a certain readiness to acknowledge that:

> [There] are things that need to be done that govern-
> ment cannot do or will not do, and things that they
> should not do, but which the spontaneous but organ-
> ized NGOs can achieve. The NGOs have arisen to
> fill this gap. They both prevent great concentration
> of power and encourage the focus of power on
> specific problems.[1]

In her inaugural speech as the President of the Carnegie Endowment for International Peace (Washington D.C., June 15, 1997), Mathews gave concise expression to the establishment's worries that the "power shift" in global affairs might weaken the elite's hold on global power structures. It is essential, she remarked, to "understand what an NGO can do in this day and age, because that terrain, too, is shifting dramatically under our feet."

A Non-Governmental Order?

The events surrounding the WTO ministerial summit in Seattle in November and December 1999 have again demonstrated that a power shift of truly global dimensions has occurred. It seems that, at least for a short time, the global economic-political domination exercised by the forces of elite globalization, operating from the foundation laid in the Bretton Woods system in 1941–44, has been shaken. The last seven years of the twentieth century, from the 1992 Earth Summit in Rio de Janeiro to the 1999 Seattle meeting, have brought about a small but growing change in global social structure. These changes demonstrate that new moral, cultural, and social forces have arisen in many human hearts, and that many of these hearts are now well connected with clearly thinking heads and powerfully active will.

What is the real agenda of the forces that developed and used the International Monetary Fund, the World Bank, and the World Trade Organization? The main critique of the Bretton Woods institutions is that they were created not in order to serve humanity as a whole, but to ensure the economic dominance of the "West versus the rest." While many individuals working in those organizations truly believe that they serve the common good, they are facing increasing public doubt and opposition. After all, it is becoming unmistakably clear that humanity at the beginning of the twenty-first century is extremely and irresponsibly unbalanced and polarized, in a state of ever-increasing economic inequality. Such imbalances must balance themselves, either rationally, through human deeds, or through upheavals, catastrophes, and wars that for the first time will be truly global.

Is this state an accident on the road to global prosperity? Or is it an unavoidable result of particular cultural-ideological assumptions? Is the democratic-liberal worldview articulated by individuals ranging from Adam Smith to Milton Friedman, Larry Summers, Thomas Friedman, and Jeffrey Sachs accidental? Who would seriously dispute today the basic cultural underpinnings of this worldview? Who would seriously deny its role in shaping the present mainstream western practical and moral social conception?

One of many representatives of this approach to globalization is Francis Fukuyama, the celebrated author of *The End of History* and *The Great Disruption*, who, in a reflection on the events in Seattle in 1999, spells out what others sometimes prefer to conceal. In an article entitled "The Left Should Love Globalization," Fukuyama writes:

> The WTO is the only international organization that stands any chance of evolving into an institution of global governance, setting rules not only for how countries will trade and invest with one another, but also for how they will deal with issues like labor standards and the environment. . . . Down the road, the WTO can become not just the advocate of economic freedom, but human freedom more generally.[2]

Similarly revealing is the following statement by Renato Ruggerio, former Director General of the WTO, in a speech delivered to the United Nations Conference on Trade and Development, referring to the WTO's efforts to develop a multilateral investment agreement: "We are writing the constitution of a single global economy."[3]

In the face of such statements by prominent leaders of elite globalization, we should listen carefully to what the leaders of the "fight over Seattle" claim when they say that:

The World Trade Organization is carrying out a
slow-motion coup d'etat over democratic governance worldwide. Unlike past trade pacts, the WTO
and its underlying agreements move far beyond
traditional commercial matters. . . . WTO provisions
set limits on the strength of countries' food safety
laws and the comprehensiveness of product labeling
policies. They forbid countries from banning products made with child labor. They can even regulate
expenditure of local tax dollars.[4]

This means that a world governance representing the interests of very small and powerful groups of people is to dictate
to the rest of humanity how to live in the three sectors of
society: how to regulate trade and investment (in economic
life); labor rights and environment (in political life); and
"human freedom more generally" (in the cultural life).

Under the title "A Non-governmental Order," the *Economist* "celebrated" the social consequences of Seattle.[5] Of
course, as a longtime protector of democracy insofar as it can
be geared to serve privileged groups and special interests, the
Economist is also well positioned to add the subtitle, "Will
NGOs democratize, or merely disrupt, global governance?"
The article, which is instructive in many respects, begins with
a well-informed estimation of the strengths and range of influence of NGOs and civil society. It describes some of the mile-
stones on civil society's path toward becoming a world power:
the "watershed" Earth Summit in Rio de Janeiro in 1992; the
"Fifty Years is Enough" campaign against the World Bank in
1994; and the sinking of the MAI draft treaty. It then follows
the campaign to outlaw land mines and some of the most
successful global campaigns against corporations (e.g., against

Nestlé's sale of powdered infant formula in poor countries, or
Monsanto's genetically modified foods and seeds). Green-
peace's victory against Royal Dutch Shell in 1995, in which the
organization prevented the corporation from discarding its
Brent Spar oil rig in the North Sea, is mentioned as a victory
that "particularly shocked business, apparently because it
demonstrated the crisis of legitimacy of transnational corporations even in cases in which the law is on their side." The *Economist* cannot but acknowledge the fact that citizens' groups are
increasingly powerful at the corporate, national, and international level. "How they have become so, and what this means,
are questions that urgently need to be addressed," the author
contends. "Are citizens' groups, as many of their supporters
claim, the first steps towards an 'international civil society'
(whatever that might be)?"

The Decentralization of Information

The *Economist* finds the globalization of communication and
information to be the main source of power for global civil
society. What this means is that the old, cherished elite ideal of
creating, maintaining, and controlling power through *secrecy*
has become increasingly difficult. Relying on the "ignorance of
the masses" has become a less certain strategy.

As long as the opponents could communicate only by tele-
phone, fax, or mail, it was prohibitively expensive to create and
maintain networks of communication. The Internet has
changed this radically. Thus, explains the *Economist*, "The
MAI was already in trouble when a draft of the text posted on
the Internet by an NGO allowed hundreds of hostile watchdog
groups to mobilize against it." And the same was true of the
organization of the Seattle trade summit, which "was disrupted

by dozens of websites which alerted everyone (except, it seems, the Seattle police) to the protests that were planned."

What an unheard of social and political catastrophe for the powers that be! Instead of welcoming a unique, unprecedented opportunity to develop global dialogue with greater parts of civil society, with fellow citizens, the *Economist* bemoans "online coalition building between environmental and citizens' groups" via e-mail. In fact, about 1,500 NGOs signed an anti-WTO protest declaration set up online by Public Citizen, a consumer-rights group. In direct contradiction of hundreds of years of elite rule, the "brute masses" can now easily access information, share knowledge, and increase their demands for equality and solidarity. In this excerpt from the same article, the writer laments the fact that knowledge concerning the abuse of human rights and the environment in the poor South can be known and used against the perpetrators in the rich North:

> More important, the Internet allows new partnerships between groups in rich and poor countries. Armed with compromising evidence of local labor practices or environmental degradation from southern NGOs, for example, activists in developed countries can attack corporations much more effectively.

A New Strategy of Decentralized Social Operation: Web, Network and a "Swarm"

A new strategy of operation, organization, and social and cultural action underlies the success of civil society. If we look more closely at its origins we discover that it is but a natural development that results from a scientific paradigmatic shift that occurred in the second half of the twentieth century. As natural science has demonstrated in many fields of research in the last century (such as physics, biology, astronomy, and ecology), Earth and the universe are living organisms, unified and informed by webs and networks of relationships, through which living information (physical, biological, or even cosmic) is constantly shared by myriad creatures. Technological advancement in communications and the dissemination of knowledge and information is based on this fact. One can say that it is a translation of a natural, planetary state of affairs to the human and social level. We are only doing in a human way what Great Nature learned to do millions of years ago: to holistically share, communicate, inter-link, and interrelate.

To those who have mastered and controlled the social world in a centralized hierarchical way in the last hundred years, this universally available communication web is felt as a real threat to their dominion. And they apply their best minds to the task of understanding the new situation and overcoming the new challenge.

The *Economist* directs our attention to a RAND corporation study (RAND is one of the most influential elite think tanks on military and strategic issues). "This phenomenon—amorphous groups of NGOs, linked online, descending on a target—has been dubbed an 'NGO swarm' in a RAND study by David Ronfeldt and John Arquilla. And such groups are awful for governments to deal with. An NGO swarm, say the RAND researchers, has no 'central leadership or command structure; it is multi-headed, impossible to decapitate.' And it can sting a victim to death." A short passage from the original cited research can make this picture clear:

> In our view, traditional warfare fits the Western paradigm symbolized by chess, where territory is very important, units are functionally specialized,

and operations proceed sequentially until checkmate. Net war, however, requires a new analytic paradigm, which, we argue, is provided by the Oriental game of Go, where there are no "fronts," offense and defense are often blurred, and fortifications and massing simply provide targets for implosive attacks. Victory is achieved not by checkmate, as there is no king to decapitate, but by gaining control of a greater amount of the "battlespace."

The medieval centralized, hierarchical principle of social organization and control was skillfully adapted to create the so-called modern, centralized and hierarchical economic, political, and cultural powers that rule most of the present global civilization. It became the foundation of a modern western domination of the planet that created the first global empires, the British world empire and, since the middle of the twentieth century, the American global empire. It is this empire, with its deep-rooted foundation in the medieval world, that civil society, or simply the spiritual-cultural sphere of human freedom, begins today to challenge.

No wonder, then, that the *Economist* finds that those international organizations created in America after World War II, while boasting that they represent the best part of a democratic world order, increasingly appear to be estranged from the wider public:

> Inter-governmental institutions such as the World Bank, the IMF, the UN agencies or the WTO have an enormous weakness in an age of NGOs: they lack political leverage. . . . Add to this the poor public image that these technocratic, faceless bureaucracies

have developed, and it is hardly surprising that they are popular targets for NGO "swarms." The WTO is only the latest to suffer.

An Uncalled-for Third is Joining the Other Two at the Social Table

After debating whether the WTO can implement the co-optation strategies successfully used by the World Bank to paralyze civil society, the *Economist* concludes its article with the following statement: "What is certain is that a new kind of actor is claiming, loudly, a seat at the table." That much is finally being understood: this guest has stopped waiting for an invitation. But while this scenario is a source of horror for the powers that be, it is a source of true hope for many of us. After all, it is a sign of a new effort to advance the truly universal human cause of our age, which, since its chaotic and misguided beginnings in the French and socialist revolutions, has been fought for in the wholly justified struggle for freedom, equality, and brotherhood. At the end of each century, and in the beginning of a new one, this impulse rises from the depth of human nature and surfaces into external of social life.

The real change since the social revolutions of the end of the eighteenth and nineteenth centuries is that from this point on each central social issue will require decision-making strategies and policies that take into account not a bipolar world (business versus states) but a tri-polar world. In a tri-polar social situation, cultural values, ethics, and meanings are no longer phrases and poetry but powerful social actors, and the needs of society *as a whole* have a far greater chance of being heard and taken care of. These needs can now often be articulated better by civil society organizations than by democratically elected but business-dominated governments.

Civil society as an emergent global power is young, and though it has already achieved a few significant public victories, it is dangerously premature to believe that it has already found or consolidated its deeper roots in modern social existence. My opinion is that in order to make a deep and lasting impact on the global social situation at the beginning of the twenty-first century, it must ally itself in full consciousness with the main thrust of the evolution of human consciousness. The more it expands its external social and cultural engagements and responsibilities, the more it should intensify its inner-directed cultural-spiritual activities and integrate them with its social commitments. Otherwise civil society inevitably runs the risk of following in the steps of other social movements in the last century that lacked a modern and wide-awake understanding of the rule of creative spiritual freedom in social life.

Notes
1. *International Herald Tribune*, January 16–17, 1999.
2. *Wall Street Journal*, December 1, 1999.
3. October 8, 1996.
4. Lori Wallach and Michelle Sforza, *The WTO: Five Years of Reasons to Resist Corporate Globalization* (New York: Seven Stories Press, 1999).
5. December 9, 1999.

Epilogue

🦋

American Renewal of
the Mysteries of the Earth

IN A LECTURE GIVEN IN DORNACH ON DECEMBER 15, 1919,[1] Rudolf Steiner referred to the nations of North America and western Europe as the carriers of the Mysteries of the Earth, or the living economic impulse out of which truly western, American, independent political and cultural-spiritual creativity could grow and prosper. These were the origins of Anglo-American economic life:

> In the customs of commercial life, whose origins lie in the national habits of the Anglo-American world, we find the ultimate outcome of what I would like to call the Mysteries of the Earth. . . . This economic life that is trying to grow has so far only managed to produce a few tiny flowers, while the cultural life and the life of rights remain alien plants the further we go westwards.

A one-sided, materialistic Anglo-American conquest of the globe was spreading the third and ultimate evil over the whole planet:

> The Anglo-American element may well achieve world dominion, but without the threefold ordering of society

this dominion will flood the world with the death of culture and the sickness of culture.

Along with Henry David Thoreau, the most remarkable representative of the American Mysteries of the Earth was the transcendentalist Ralph Waldo Emerson. He was a true planetary and cosmic gardener, an industrialist of imaginative and living thinking—an exemplar of the greatest gifts that the Great Spirit, in conjunction with the Earth Mother, bestows on human beings in the western and northern nations. Emerson is the representative of a whole new spiritual, American wave of inspiration, the first to fully translate the fruits of the fertile American continent into modern acts of creative will and imaginative thinking. The same tremendous creative American energy that J. P. Morgan, John D. Rockefeller, and others realized in their mechanical, industrial, and social innovations and achievements, Emerson embodied spiritually.

The living picture of Emerson—so finely painted by Robert Richardson in his excellent book, *Emerson: The Mind on Fire*—is the picture of the never-tiring and ever-industrious craftsman and industrialist of the spirit: gathering, distributing, mining, melting, and transubstantiating the farthest and deepest treasures of universal human culture; molding and shaping in each moment a new intellect, knowledge, memory, fantasy, and language, to create entirely new foundations for future western culture. Emerson's uniqueness lies in the fact that his soul and spiritual faculties are thoroughly penetrated and transformed by means of his creative and dynamic will power. Emerson said of himself, aptly, "I am a rocket manufacturer," that is, a modern, Michaelic knight in the best Arthurian sense, whose mission is to achieve the holy grail of the West by means of the full spiritualization of the embodied bodily faculties: will power, instinct, desire, habit, fantasy, sense perception, and objective scientific thought.

It is, above all, the faculty of spiritualized instinct, so difficult to achieve—the faculty that true representatives of European spirit, such as Goethe, Nietzsche, and Wolfram von Eschenbach (author of *Parsifal*) were striving to develop—that was Emerson's inborn capacity:

> As the traveler who has lost his way, throws his reins on his horse's neck, and trusts to the instinct of the animal to find his road, so must we do with the divine animal who carries us through the world. For if in any manner we can stimulate this instinct, new passages are opened for us into nature, the mind flows into and through things hardest and the highest, and the metamorphosis is possible.[2]

Emerson's experience of the productive role of the imagination in inventing, creating, and shaping nature, culture, and society, his understanding of the nature of science as the highest poetic production and of language as "fossil poetry," planted the fertile seeds from which the renewal of the living mysteries of Anglo-American economy is nourished in each age:

> This insight, which expresses itself by what is called Imagination, is a very high sort of seeing, which does not come by study, but by the intellect being where and what it sees, by sharing the path, or circuit of things through forms, and so making them translucid to others.[3]

As Rudolf Steiner indicated above, the western "Mysteries"—
that is, the western-northern sources of spiritual inspirations—
have been known in past ages to be "the Mysteries of the
Earth." In those mysteries, Earth was always grasped as a
living, sentient, and spiritual being in its own right, part of a
cosmic, intelligent brotherhood, represented in the visible and
invisible, and in the planets, suns, and constellations of the infinite universe. "Economy" has a precise meaning in these
mysteries: adapting social life as a whole—first and foremost in
agricultural and industrial production, consumption, and
commerce—to the great planetary and cosmic cycle of life.

These mysteries also gave rise to uniquely western inspirations for politics and cultural life, for they point out the
preciousness of earthly life and the gift of birth, life, and
mortality. Only awareness of the value of this gift can inspire a
shared sense of freedom and brotherhood, as well as cooperation, as well as divide fairly the abundant gifts which loving
Mother Earth and the great Universal Spirit bestow on all life.
In the western and northern countries, the Mysteries of the
Earth inspire an ecological and hence brotherly and communal
economic sense, which in its turn naturally shapes egalitarian
political and cultural-spiritual social life, locally, and globally.
Tri-sector society grows in this way as naturally as a living tree
or plant, from below, out of the living soil of local economic
practices in the first sector, to inspire the second (political) and
third (cultural) sectors with true human values.

Western (today mainly American) "initiation" into these
Mysteries operates on all three levels of "social economy":
economically, politically, and culturally. It was not by accident
that toward the end of the twentieth century, as part of the
evolving, beneficent Michaelic time spirit—global, local,
creative, daring—that mature visions and conscious articula-

tions of the true, spiritualized essence of American economy emerged in many ways. One of the most significant appeared in the notion of "natural capitalism," developed in the 1980s at the Rocky Mountain Institute and published in *Natural Capitalism: Creating the Next Industrial Revolution.*

According to the principles of "natural capitalism," the four principles of natural capitalism as a new business model are as follows: a radical increase in the productivity of resource use to maximize energy and productivity; a shift to biologically inspired production (or biomimicry), with closed energy loops, and no waste or toxicity; a turn away from simply making and selling things to provide the services that the product used to provide; and a reinvestment in natural and human capital— returning energy back to the source of that energy and the individuals who benefit from it.[4]

Here we find the beginning of an independent expression of the economic ideals of the modern western Mysteries of the Earth, and we can realize the truth of Steiner's indications that such an independent, western economic life harbors an original transformation of the whole social structure. The term "economy," as understood in terms of natural capitalism, is a seed of a new conception of western civilization, because such economy brings forth the stems, branches, leaves, and flowers of political and cultural life as naturally as a flower grows in its wholeness from healthy seed and fertile soil. Legislation, human rights, arts and culture, and religion and sciences receive unmistakably ecological, communal, and human meaning in this economy, as demonstrated by David Korten's notion of a living communal economy for a living Earth—a powerful, specifically American strategy to aid civil society's efforts for social renewal. In America, all that we need to do is to listen carefully and attentively to the beat of Mother Earth's heart, in order to find, in one way or another, a suitable entry point to fruitful social life. This life will then grow and branch out into all social domains with natural-human power.

The American economy, grasped in this sense, bears in itself the sources of vital cultural and spiritual reality, because it is rooted in the unique American talent to use the generously offered riches and gifts of great Mother Nature—the spouse of the Great Cosmic Spirit—for the physical well-being and welfare of all humans, races, and nations of Earth. In America this is a direct reality, experienced whenever creative and courageous people do not try to imitate decadent European and Asian ways of life, but, assimilating the best that European and Asian cultures can offer, use their unique capabilities to create an imaginative American economy, politics, and culture. This happens when the individualizing urgency of the experience of human mortality comes together with the riches of our living planet. If they are true to themselves, the political and cultural ideals of the West are fresh and non-traditional outgrowths of the inspirations flowing out of such existential economic activity.

The Mysteries of the Earth inspire us today to experience that we are daughters and sons of Earth, on which we can stand fully upright and expand our reach to a mysteriously sacred universe above. This is the original western experience of our humanity in the present epoch, which we must develop fully. Earth bestows on us the fruits of individuation, and we can globalize them, bring their benefits to all humans on Earth, and carry them to the far reaches of the starry cosmos. Individualized life takes place in the rapid stream of time, while longevity increases with the accelerating flow of innovations and events. Life is a perpetual process of becoming, evolution, and transformation, rhythmically metamorphosing itself

through evolution and involution. This is the unique contribution of western culture to global culture.

Our self-consciousness, individuality, mortality, and acceleration spur us to constantly improve and develop the physical foundations and conditions of all economic, political, and cultural aspects of life. It is, therefore, an entirely new, mortalized-immortalized (individuated), planetary, and cosmic economy that comes to meet us as we move westward, just as Asia's eternal spirituality meets us as an ageless, sublime spiritual wisdom, the farther east we go.

Through this process, an ideal "Europe" is resurrected from its twentieth-century grave, wherever and whenever western and eastern life meet and complement each other. The secret of a wholly new global "center" is beginning to manifest itself in this way, in millions of scattered seed-centers in which true global economy, polity, and culture emerge. In this way, an organic development of a holistic conception of global human society becomes discernible, in which new foundations for the economy, polity, and culture—which will become increasingly influential at the beginning of the twenty-first century—are laid:

1. **New awareness of the living planet and ecology become a foundation for a new economy.** This new awareness expresses itself first in organic, biodynamic, and eco-agricultural practices, but then expands naturally to embrace new forms of handling practical economic activities. Today, a variety of practices of cooperative, decentralized, associative, and community-based economies are developing around the globe, where cooperation instead of cutthroat competition is the basis for the relationships between producers, consumers, and traders. There are also

many new ways of dealing with money, including alternative and community-based banking and responsible and ethical investment.

2. **New awareness of human suffering and rights becomes a foundation for a new polity.** Alternative understanding of the role of the state, governments, and the law is beginning to impact local, national, international, and global governance. Especially innovative are the new conceptions of the state's role as mediator between market forces and the forces of culture. Instead of controlling both and interfering with their practical business, the human-social element of the state becomes more understood and attention is directed more to the role of mediating, communicating, balancing, and harmonizing the diverse and often contrary pressures of economy and culture.

3. **New awareness of childhood and education becomes a foundation for a new culture.** This means that substantial advancement is being made in understanding children's development and unique needs, and seeing how much of modern culture is so often inimical to the physical, mental, and spiritual health of our children. This brings with it great changes and creative new approaches in education. The administration of the sciences, arts, and medical and justice issues will become increasingly person- and community-centered. Behaviorism, which reached its maximum cultural and social significance in the 1960s in the "culture of despair," and bio-sociology and neo-Darwinian sociology, though still powerful, are being replaced in many places with humanistic, even transpersonal and holistic approaches to education and medicine, the arts, and our understanding of the significance of culture in forming human life as a whole.

American Earthly and Cosmic Biology
Two significant and original results of the modern, specifically American-western initiation into the new Mysteries of the Earth can be mentioned here, because they hold tremendous creative potential, for good and ill, for the future of global civilization. The first expresses itself in the exploration of outer space, and the second in the exploration of the secrets of biological life.

Physical exploration of Earth's atmosphere and outer space is a justified projection and expansion of the age of Earth exploration and discovery. The science and technology that make this possible, themselves results of the new earthly economic powers, allow for the first time the physically incarnated human being to raise her mind and heart to the stars and become a free citizen of the cosmos, while standing firmly grounded on the living earth below. With the living earth under her feet, she can raise her full earthly humanity upward and celebrate western creativity and dynamism, experiencing the world of the stars and the cosmos as a rightful extension of a living earthly home. Thanks to such largely American economic, political, and cultural ideals and capabilities—President Kennedy's moon project is a exemplary study case of this—human beings saw the living, vibrant Earth for the first time from outer space, and began to experience their responsibility for this precious global home.

As a result, a powerful rejuvenation of the Mysteries of the Earth streamed to our planet from outer space, as we realized for the first time our planet's uniqueness in the cosmos. An indescribable sense of loving care for Earth, caused by this "intimacy from afar," was internalized by millions all over the planet in the 1960s and '70s. In this manner, America led and inspired the expansion of earthly science and technology, and became a foundation for a new expansion of consciousness and a deepening of the moral-social commitment of the West to the welfare of humanity as a whole. As we saw above, this is one of the strongest inspirations that animates civil society's moral call for the awakening of global conscience.

With this new vision, Mother Earth and her myriads of living children, spread so majestically around us were illuminated "from above"—even though they had been lost to us in the high days of twentieth-century materialism as western humanity strove to conquer, manipulate, and devour the planet. Many were awakened from their materialistic slumber, the nihilism of the "culture of despair," as they experienced with shock and shame to what extent we in the West have treated Earth and her peoples as a mere source for cheap raw materials and human labor. The gift of this perspective is undeniably one of the most important contributions of the new Mysteries of the Earth (in which is found the economic source of modern science and technology) to the planetary social initiation of human consciousness in our time.

The link between outer space exploration and the new consciousness of the living planet as an organism is demonstrated best in the inspiration that led James Lovelock to postulate his "Gaia hypothesis." The hypothesis originated with NASA's research in preparation for a possible future Mars mission. Fritjof Capra has told this fascinating story in his book *The Web of Life*. Realizing that what Mars lacks is a living, self-regulating atmosphere, Lovelock begun to wonder how Earth itself had developed one:

The Earth's atmosphere was an extraordinary and unstable mixture of gases, yet I knew that it was constant in composition over quite long periods of time. Could it be that life on Earth not only made the atmosphere, but also regulated it—keeping it at a constant composition, and at a level favorable for organisms?[5]

The new Mysteries of the Earth began to speak again in the 1960s. They will increase their revelation from now on in each new century, until Earth will once more be experienced by humans in its full living, ensouled, and spiritual splendor:

Consider Gaia theory as an alternative to the conventional wisdom that sees the Earth as a dead planet made of inanimate rocks, ocean, and atmosphere, and merely inhabited by life. Consider it as a real system, comprising all of life and all of its environment tightly coupled so as to form a self-regulating entity.[6]

This radical transformation of our scientific understanding of the being of Earth is a founding act, an original seed-point, out of which immeasurable future scientific, artistic, religious, and social developments are springing forth. However, in order to reach this goal, much must still be transformed in our thinking and understanding of the nature of life on Earth and in the universe.

In his book *Investigations*, Stuart Kauffman relates a conversation in the summer of 1997 between Vice President Al Gore and prominent American scientists, who met in the wake of NASA's attempt to formulate the science of "astrobiology," a discipline that would seek "to understand the origin, evolution, and characteristics of life anywhere in the universe." The group discussed the discovery of a form of algae that had been found on Mars. Gore asked the scientists what might be the

least and most interesting results should this algae be indeed
Martian in origin.

The scientists agreed that the least interesting result would
be if the algae's composition was just like Earth's. The most
interesting, they thought, would be if the algae was radically
different. That, says Kauffman, raised a host of intriguing
possibilities: that life in other parts of the universe would "not
be improbable," indeed perhaps abundant; that we are not
alone and that the universe continues to create life; that we
might be at the beginning of a different kind of biology—a
cosmic biology, an "astrobiology." Kauffman writes:

> Many of us, including Mr. Gore, while maintaining
> skepticism about the Mars rock itself, spoke at that
> meeting about the spiritual impact of the discovery of
> life elsewhere in the universe. The general consensus
> was that such a discovery, linked to the sense of
> membership in a creative universe, would alter how we
> see ourselves and our place under all the suns. I find it
> a gentle, thrilling, quiet, and transforming vision.[7]

Taken in this sense, Kauffman's story—like Lovelock's
rediscovery of Gaia, the new social-economic practice of
"natural capitalism," or the Northern conception of "deep
ecology" developed by the Norwegian thinker Arne Naess,
among so many others—is historically symptomatic. Sympto-
matically, Kauffman hints at America's global and cosmic
vocation in this age, which is *the renewal of the Mysteries of
the Earth*.

Global civil society needs the new forces of inspiration that
stream from the spiritualized scientific, technological, ecological, and economic depth of these new Earth mysteries. The

fulfillment of America's global responsibility depends on our ability, all around the globe, to be inspired and guided by its light and life.

Notes

1. "The Michael Impulse," Lecture XII from *The Mysteries of Light, of Space, and of the Earth.* See www.bobnancy.com/bobnancy.html (viewed on October 13, 2003).
2. Ralph Waldo Emerson, "The Poet," from *Self-Reliance and Other Essays* (Mineola, N.Y.: Dover Publications, 1993).
3. Ibid.
4. Paul Hawken, Amory Lovins, and L. Hunter Lovins, *Natural Capitalism: Creating the Next Industrial Revolution* (Boston: Little, Brown and Co., 1999).
5. Fritjof Capra, *The Web of Life* (New York: Doubleday, 1997), pp. 227–8.
6. Ibid., pp. 102–3.
7. Stuart A. Kauffman, *Investigations* (Oxford: New York: Oxford University Press, 2000).

About the Author

৵

Jesaiah Ben-Aharon is co-founder of Activists for Israeli Civil Society (ICS), a member of the Global Network for Three-folding. ICS fosters the heritage and values of universal and progressive Judaism as a foundation for the self-organization of civil society in Israel, and works toward the implementation of social threefoldinig in the state of Israel and the world. More information is available at www.civilsociety.co.il/eng. He is the author of two books, both published by Temple Lodge Books in 2000: *The Spiritual Event of the Twentieth Century: An Imagination of the Occult Significance of the 12 Years 1933–4 in the Light of Spiritual Science* and *The New Experience of the Supersensible*.